CHRISTIANITY AND THE TEENAGE THINKER

Christianity and the Teenage Thinker

*Morning Assemblies for
Secondary Schools*

DAVID SELLICK

© *A. R. Mowbray & Co. Ltd.* 1969

Printed in Great Britain by
Alden & Mowbray Ltd
at the Alden Press, Oxford

SBN 264 64502 2

First Published in 1969

CONTENTS

Preface   ix

BEATITUDES   1
  1. Introductory   3
  2. The Poor   5
  3. The Mourners   7
  4. The Meek   9
  5. The Hungry and Thirsty   11
  6. The Merciful   13
  7. The Pure in Heart   15
  8. The Peacemakers   17
  9. The Persecuted   19

FEASTS AND FASTS   21
  1. All Saints and All Souls   23
  2. Christmas   25
  3. Epiphany   27
  4. The Conversion of Saint Paul   29
  5. The Beginning of Lent   32
  6. Ash Wednesday   34
  7. Messiah (i)   37
  8. Messiah (ii)   39
  9. Messiah (iii)   41
  10. Messiah (iv)   43
  11. Messiah (v)   45
  12. Messiah (vi)   47
  13. Easter   49

14. Ascension Day   51
15. Whitsun   53

THE LORD'S PRAYER   55
1. 'Our Father'   57
2. 'Which art in Heaven'   59
3. 'Hallowed be Thy Name'   61
4. 'Thy Kingdom come . . .'   63
5. 'Give us our daily bread'   65
6. 'Forgive us our trespasses . . .'   67
7. 'Lead us not into temptation'   69
8. 'But deliver us from evil'   72
9. 'For Thine is the Kingdom'   74

PARABLES   77
1. Be Prepared   79
2. Excuses   81
3. Forgiveness   83
4. Foundations   85
5. Last first, first last   87
6. Lost and Found   90
7. Prayer   92
8. The Speck and the Plank   95
9. Talents   98
10. Total Selfishness   101

SAINTS   105
1. Saint Matthew   107
2. Saint Francis of Assisi   109
3. Saint Luke, the Doctor   111
4. King Alfred the Great   113
5. Saint John the Baptist   115
6. Saint Nicolas   117
7. Innocents' Day   119
8. Saint Paul   122
9. Saint Valentine   125

10.	Mary, Mother of Jesus	127
11.	Saint Peter (i) The Coward	129
12.	Saint Peter: (ii) 'The Rock'	132
13.	Saint Mark	134
14.	Saint Alban	136
15.	Saint Swithin	138

THOUGHT PROVOKERS | 141

1.	Angels	143
2.	The Bible	145
3.	Christian Aid	147
4.	The Constancy of God	149
5.	Daniel, the Courageous	151
6.	Examinations	154
7.	Faith	156
8.	Friendship	159
9.	Race	161
10.	The Sea	163
11.	Vocation	165
12.	War	168

Acknowledgements | 170

PREFACE

The purpose of these 'Assemblies' is to stimulate the minds of Secondary School pupils into thinking seriously about Christianity and themselves. While no claim for originality of material is made, what this book aims at is the presentation of problems real to young people in a way that can be readily understood by young people. The writings of even the most popular of paperback theologians need to be predigested and re-stated with young people in mind. Many teachers will easily recognise the extent and limitations of my own reading.

The Assemblies were presented in a Secondary Selective School over a period of three years in more or less the form given here. Hymns are always a problem. The ones offered here are all to be found in *Songs of Praise* but in many cases any one of a particular school's repertoire would be as appropriate or as irrelevant. The hymns that *are* relevant are found in most hymnaries. The time factor is a problem too and these suggestions were tailored to fit a fairly rigid programme. This will acount for the complete absence of a prayer in one or two cases where it was felt the music somewhat compensated for the lack of verbal expression. The Biblical readings are from the New English Bible (*N.T.*) and the Revised Standard Version (*O.T.*).

Hardly a week passed without some unsolicited reaction, usually appreciative but not always so, from one or two pupils and very often from colleagues. My gratitude is due to my wife for two reasons; first she was the 'pilot audience' as each assembly journeyed from home to school, and revisions at this stage saved from many a doctrinal error and lapse into incomprehensibility, and second my wife is my typist.

DAVID SELLICK

BEATITUDES

1. Introductory

By saying 'fight the good fight' the author of the hymn recognises that it is not going to be easy to practise Christianity. It is going to be a struggle. But we have Christ, his example and his teaching to provide us with a path.

Saint Matthew has collected all Jesus' most essential teaching into one great sermon which is known as the Sermon on the Mount'. This begins with the Beatitudes, which are a number of phrases which begin with the words 'Blessed are the . . . .'

I want us to examine these Beatitudes in some detail.

First of all we must look at the word 'Blessed'. As so often happens we are hampered by a translation problem. We say 'Blessed are the . . . ', but there is no verb in the Greek sentence. So the Beatitudes are exclamations. But the Greek is only a translation of a Hebrew word *'ashere'* which means 'O the bliss of . . . .'

The Beatitudes are not promises of what will happen in the future they are congratulations on a special sort of happy contentedness which people have now, in the present.

It is hard to find a satisfactory translation. In the 1920s the phrase "How ripping!' was used. This gets near the idea but is forty years out of date. One could say 'How lucky', but there is no element of chance in this situation. Actually it is not very fashionable to be seen to be very happy in these days, so we lack a really fashionable word for 'bliss'. Perhaps that is the first lesson we can learn from the Beatitudes, to look for happiness and try to get as

3

much enjoyment as possible out of every situation we find ourselves in; to make the most out of every moment we are alive, to be an optimist. Maybe we shall be able to force a new word to be fashionable, one which brings 'blessed' right up to date.

Let us pray:

O God, the giver of all good gifts, we thank thee for all the many blessings which we have. Give us always contented minds, cheerful hearts, and ready wills, so that we may spend and be spent in the service of others, after the example of him who gave his life a ransom for many, our Lord and Master, Jesus Christ. Amen.

A Book of Prayers for Schools

2. The Poor

'Blessed are the poor for theirs is the kingdom of heaven,' said Jesus in the 'Sermon on the Mount.' Dr Johnson said, 'Poverty is a great enemy to human happiness; it certainly destroys liberty . . .'

We are more likely to think of poverty as being something to be avoided rather than a circumstance in which to be blessed. But there are one or two aspects of being poor which do in some measure compensate for the material deprivation.

The author of the words of this morning's hymn is well aware of some of the advantages of poverty, hunger and sorrow.

HYMN: *How sweet the name of Jesus sounds in a believer's ear.*

Henry VII is praised by historians for having the sense to see that if he was to make the House of Tudor strong, influential and permanent he had to accumulate wealth. Very few people are influential in the world today who are not also very rich. It is the richer nations who determine world policy, not the poorer ones who might in fact lead to much greater world happiness.

A poor person has no power, no prestige, no influence, he is often oppressed and pushed around by the richer men. But in spite of this he may retain his integrity, he may be loyal, he may have a sincere belief in God. He has no help on earth; he is easily able to see that abundance of material possessions do not bring happiness. He recognises a sense of need. Jesus said it was very difficult for the rich to follow his teaching. This is so because people who have great wealth find it takes all their time to look after it so they have no time for anything or anybody else. We all depend so much upon chance for our happiness. Lady

5

Luck is very fickle; but a way to become independent of luck and chance is to depend upon God. Strange isn't it? The way to true independence comes through complete dependence. This is a paradox; something which sounds wrong but is really absolutely right.

The Kingdom of Heaven which the poor have is no earthly kingdom which depends on wealth for its existence; it is doing the will of God; those who do the will of God belong to the Kingdom of Heaven.

These aspects of poverty we can try, preferably without extremes, to have in our lives, and so we shall be assured of genuine happiness. The poor are aware of ultimate dependence upon God; they have nothing material to lose and they can distinguish between what is material and temporal; that is, not much good and not likely to last long, and what is spiritual and eternal, that is good and will last for ever. In this respect blessed indeed are the poor.

Let us pray:

> O Saviour Christ, who dost lead them to immortal blessed-ness, who commit themselves to thee: Grant that we, being weak presume not to trust in ourselves, but may always have thee before our eyes, to follow thee, our guide; that thou, who only knowest the way, mayst lead us to our heavenly desires. To thee with the Father and the Holy Ghost be glory for ever. Amen.

Primer, 1545 (adapted)

3. The Mourners

Everbody feels sorry for people who are unhappy or sad. 'Quite right, too', we say when somebody says 'Blessed are they that mourn for they shall be comforted.' But who are the mourners that Jesus has in mind here? This is what we will try to discover this morning.

HYMN: *O God our help in ages past.*

No-one likes to mourn or to be sad but there are four ways in which sadness can produce good results. It is a mistake to believe that we should seek sadness or that we should thank God for sending us sadness but it's a fact that in the natural course of things we can discover something through being sad:

First, when some frightful disaster strikes a person and he is very sorrowful he either finds great comfort in his religion or he loses his faith altogether. So sorrow gives an opportunity for the sincerity of our belief to be tested. If we have been superficial and shallow in our attitude to God then this superficiality will be exposed; if our faith in God is deep and sincere we will find our religion a great comfort.

Second, sometimes it is better to undergo some hardship to achieve a worthwhile goal. You may be sorry to give up doing certain things to concentrate upon school work to achieve certain objectives. Sometimes the goal is very distant; and the more distant the goal the more difficult it is to forgo immediate pleasure, but the present sorrow is always compensated by the future pleasure.

Third, we can all do well to be sorrowful on occasions for the rather poor state the world is in; there is so much unnecessary suffering in the world for which we each, as human beings, must bear some responsibility. Genuine sorrow here must lead to a resolve to do something about it.

Fourth, we do well to be sorrowful about our own shortcomings. There are very few of us who do not admit being a little less good than we really ought to be. Realising this, we can try to improve ourselves.

Then all who mourn are to be 'comforted'. This does not mean soothing words, something soft and 'wishy-washy' but 'made strong'; we talk of military 'forts'. This is the sort of comfort which supports us when we are down-hearted and drives us forward to do something about it, to improve the state of the world, to make ourselves better people.

Let us pray:

O Jesus Christ, strong Son of God, friend of the weak, who dost lead thy servants to battle against disease and sin; make us brave in following thee; make us worthy of the hosts who have striven in thy name for right and freedom. Teach us to hate all oppression and kindle in our hearts a passion for justice and kindness. Make us ready to succour the weak, with hearts that sympathise and hands that help. Give us thine own courage that we may not falter in thy service, but be worthy of thee, for thy Name's sake. Amen.

HUGH MARTIN: *A Book of Prayers for Schools*

4. The Meek

HYMN: *Breathe on me, Breath of God.*

A complete lack of courage is called cowardice; too much courage is called recklessness or stupidity. Courage therefore comes half-way between the two.

The word 'meek' in the statement 'Blessed are the meek' is a similar half-way-word. The one extreme is a complete lack of spirit, or 'guts'; an apparant inability to feel the least bit strongly about anything. The other extreme is where somebody feels passionately about everything, who loses his temper at the least provocation, or no provocation at all.

Meekness means feeling anger for the right reasons, against the right persons, in the right manner, at the right moment and for the right length of time.

People trying to find fault with the character of Christ refer to the account of his overturning the money-changer's tables and driving them out of the temple. But here Jesus was angry for the right reasons—the money-changers were making large profits out of people coming to the temple and having to exchange Roman money for Jewish Temple Currency; against the right persons,—it was only the money-changers he drove away not their clients and in the right manner,—it was no good saying 'Look here chaps, this is not really right you know', because they would laugh, they had to see that Jesus felt really strongly about the abuse; at the right moment,—it was Passover time and no doubt the money-changers were looking for big profits, and for the right length of time—as soon as the money-changers were gone Jesus healed people coming to him and taught in the temple.

9

To be right, anger must be self-less. It must be an anger which is not destructive, but aimed at reforming. The world would be a poorer place without righteous anger, the anger of the meek, such as was felt by Lord Shaftesbury, William Wilberforce, Elizabeth Fry, and is being felt by men and women who feel strongly today about many injustices that still exist in the world.

Blessed are the meek for they shall inherit the earth. By being self-controlled and still feeling strongly they feel at peace with themselves. But more important, there is great power in being meek because others can see the meek feeling strongly in a completely unselfish way, being angry without losing their tempers. It is through this power that the meek inherit the earth and galvanise others into action as well as themselves.

Let us pray:

O God the Father of the forsaken, who dost teach us that love towards man is the bond of perfectness, and the imitation of thyself: Open our eyes and touch our hearts that we may see and do the things which belong to our peace. Strengthen us in the work which we have undertaken: give us wisdom, perseverance, faith, and zeal, and in thine own time and according to thy pleasure prosper the issue; for the love of thy Son Jesus Christ. Amen.

LORD SHAFTESBURY

5. The Hungry and Thirsty

As he was starting out on a journey, a stranger ran up, and, kneeling before him, asked, 'Good Master, what must I do to win eternal life?' Jesus said to him, 'Why do you call me good? No-one is good except God alone. You know the commandments: 'Do not murder; do not commit adultery; do not steal; do not give false evidence; do not defraud; honour your father and mother.' 'But Master,' he replied, 'I have kept all these since I was a boy.' Jesus looked straight at him; his heart warmed to him, and he said, 'One thing you lack: go, sell everything you have, and give to the poor, and you will have riches in heaven; and come, follow me.' At these words his face fell and he went away with a heavy heart; for he was a man of great wealth.

Mark 10.17–22

'Blessed are they which do hunger and thirst after righteousness, for they shall be filled.' A person who reads a lot is said to devour many books. A model pupil laps up information. A keen student thirsts for knowledge. The author of this morning's hymn thinks in terms of eating and drinking when considering God and religion.

HYMN: *The King of love my shepherd is.*

Hunger and thirst really meant something to the people who first heard the words of this Beatitude. Everybody in Palestine lived just about on the level of subsistence. Unemployment for a man, even for a day, meant no food for him, his wife and family. In the parched wilderness thirst too could be very real if a sandstorm caught you miles from a well with an empty water bottle. The rich man of the story we began with was interested in righteousness but he did not hunger and thirst after it in the sense that he regarded it as absolutely vital that he was satisfied in this respect. This is a very important point. If you are going to be a Christian you have got to do it absolutely; no compromise will do. The Beatitude also reminds us that success is not the main thing, it is the fact that you have tried hard. Thomas à Kempis said 'Man sees the deed but God sees the intention.'

What is righteousness? Three things:

One: justice for oneself; social justice for all men.

Two: doing one's duty to God and to men.

Three: justifying one's own existence upon earth; justification being by faith, that is, belief in God, and by 'works' that is by doing good in the world.

Those who hunger and thirst after righteousness shall be 'filled',—filled with satisfaction; a perfect contentment. That does not mean that you do seven good deeds a day for three years and you are there; but that this state is the consequence of continually hungering and thirsting after righteousness.

Let us pray:

O Lord our God, in whose hands is the issue of all things, who requirest from thy stewards not success, but faithfulness: Give us such faith in thee, and in thy sure purposes, that we measure not our lives by what we have done, or failed to do, but by our obedience to thy will; through Jesus Christ our Lord, who endured the Cross, and now liveth and reigneth with thee and the Holy Ghost, for ever and ever. Amen.

G. W. BRIGGS; *Daily Prayer*

6. The Merciful

Kindness is a quality universally admired in our society today. God is often spoken of as being kind and merciful. Our hymn describes these attributes of God.

HYMN: *There's a wideness in God's mercy.*

'Blessed are the merciful, for they shall obtain mercy.'

You can show mercy in two ways; first of all you can let somebody off when you are in a position to punish him; secondly you can be merciful by not taking advantage of anyone, by understanding his position, in fact by being kind. The Old Testament is full of remarks concerning the mercy of God. In fact in Psalm 136 it states that the 'mercy of God endures for ever' thirty-six times! But in the Old Testament mercy is a quality only God was expected to have like being infinite or eternal. Ordinary people were not expected to be infinite, eternal, or exceptionally merciful, except of course to their friends.

Jesus spoke of all men having this quality of mercy. The parable of the Good Samaritan shows a Gentile being kind, showing mercy, to a Jew. Shakespeare also had high praise of the quality of mercy which he talks of dropping 'as the gentle rain upon the just and the unjust.'

Societies which have not been touched by Christianity seem to lack this quality altogether. Certain primitive West African tribes considered twins very bad luck to the extent that the babies were killed, put in a pot and removed from the hut through a hole in the wall which was immediately blocked up. At the time of Christ slaves were very poorly treated; they could be whipped or branded at the whim of their masters. Greeks and Romans exposed sickly babies on the mountainside to die, especially girls. The misfortune of others was the source of amusement for many peoples around the Middle East at the time of Christ.

This was the background of thought when Jesus said 'Blessed are the merciful for they shall obtain mercy.'

There are five ways in which being merciful makes us better people, more Christ-like in our attitude:

First, if you show mercy you cannot be thinking only of yourself; you must be thinking of another individual.

Second, mercy doesn't just stop at thinking about another, it involves doing something you don't call somebody 'kind' if he carefully steps over another person who has fallen and broken a leg or something. He didn't inflict the injury so he takes no blame for its occurrence. But his action was not kind. It is kind when that person assists the fallen. He shows mercy because he puts himself in the other's shoes and imagines the pain that the other is suffering.

Third, a merciful man is tolerant because he tries to see things from another's point of view.

Fourth, a merciful person is forgiving because he can see how in a similar situation he himself may have done a similar deed. So he does not roundly condemn but understands and tries to help.

Fifth, being truly merciful means that the help you give is much more effective because you try to understand the feelings of the person receiving help. You know how people can make you feel awful when they help in a very patronising manner. If they were merciful their help would be much more acceptable and valuable.

Let us pray:

Grant us, O Lord God, the glory of praying with Jesus on the Cross, by praying for our enemies, and by forgiving them that wrong or despitefully use us; that we ourselves may better deserve the gift of thy glorious pardon; through Jesus Christ our Lord. Amen.

Daily Prayer

7. The Pure in Heart

Occasionally, very occasionally, we find a hymn in which all the ideas expressed agree with our own ideas and the words of which we find for the most part understandable. This morning we are to sing such a hymn. It only needs explaining that 'meet' in the last line of the last verse means suitable or fitting. 'A temple suitable for thee!

HYMN: *Blessed are the pure in heart.*

Degrees of purity are discussed daily in the chemistry laboratory. The English Staff will extol the virtues of purity of language. In the workshops impurity in metals will be blamed for faults in various jobs.

Many things are expected to be pure. The Jews of Christ's day thought the purity of people was to be achieved by much ritual washing and the avoidance of certain types of food.

Jesus said, in effect, 'Blow all this washing and scrubbing, picking and choosing, just see that the motives you have for all you do are pure; make sure that your reasons for doing a thing are good.' 'Blessed are the pure in heart for they shall see God.' Donations to charity to avoid paying tax will not raise God's opinion of a person. Doing good so that friends and neighbours can see how good and kind you are does not assure you of a place in heaven. God is interested to see people do good because they *care for others*; because they *care*. People who go regularly to church for no other reason than to impress the neighbours with their piety would do better to stay at home. Those who go to worship God and for that reason alone please God.

15

Take time occasionally to check the motives for the things you do. Make sure too that you check your own motives and do not go round saying that other people do things for the wrong motives until you are absolutely certain about it, which you never can be.

Let us pray:

O God, our Father, before we go out on our duties and the tasks of this day, we ask thee to direct, to control, and to guide us all through its hours.

Grant that today we may never for one moment forget Thy presence.

Grant that we may take no step, and that we may come to no decision, without thy guidance, and that, before we act, we may ever seek to find thy will for us.

Be on our lips, that we may speak no evil word.

Be in our eyes, that they may never linger on any forbidden thing.

Be on our hands, that we may do our own work with diligence, and serve the needs of others with eagerness.

Be in our minds, that no soiled or bitter thought may gain an entry to them.

Be in our hearts, that they may be warm with love for thee, and for our fellow-men.

Help us to begin, to continue, and to end this day in thee: through Jesus Christ our Lord. Amen.

WILLIAM BARCLAY

8. The Peace-makers

Everybody looks forward to the time when the whole world will be at peace. Peace in Vietnam, peace in Nigeria, industrial peace. . . , everywhere there seems to be a cry for the cessation of hostilities which we call peace. When Jesus spoke the words 'Blessed are the peace-makers, for they shall be called the sons of God,' there was in fact peace in this sense throughout most of the known world. Maybe we have missed something; perhaps the word peace has lost some of it's positive meaning over the years. To have a full understanding of this Beatitude, we must try to recapture the original meaning of the word.

HYMN: *Thy Kingdom come! on bended knee.*

The first point to note is that Jesus speaks not of peace-lovers but peace-makers. You know how we hear parents say: 'Oh, anything for a bit of peace and quiet!' They are lovers of peace who in order to obtain peace give way on whatever question is bothering the disturber of their peace. But peace-makers are those who make deliberate efforts to bring peace into their lives and the world around them. Peace here means not merely cessation of hostilities but prosperity and happiness. This is why the rabbis of Jesus' day taught their pupils the greeting 'Peace be unto you.'

People can have peace in this positive sense in three ways and in each case the synonym 'right relationship' could be used:

First, one can be at peace within oneself. Most of the day we are torn between two or more things; it is significant that we use the word 'torn' which suggests that somebody or something gets hurt. This morning I was 'torn' between my desire to stay in bed and my duty to come to school. If I were to develop peace within myself I should not have this inner conflict, I would simply do what I knew to be right. To be peace-makers ourselves we need to work out our theories of life so that we can quickly come to decisions without internal conflict.

Second, and this is a very good way of achieving the first, we must be at peace with God. In other words we should try to maintain a clear conscience. If we know what is right and do it we are making peace with God and within ourselves.

Third, we must have a right relationship with others, our fellowmen. In this third aspect, of course, we are putting into practice the results of the other two aspects of peace-making. Being a peace-maker does not merely mean not picking quarrels with our fellows but positively seeking their best interests; doing what you can for others wherever opportunities arise; in fact loving your neighbour as yourself. The world is made up of individuals living in relationship with others. When all the individuals are peace-makers then there will be peace in Vietnam, Nigeria, Rhodesia, the docks—everywhere; then we shall all be sons of God. This phrase 'son of' so common in the Bible, son of consolation, sons of Thunder, son of righteousness—arises because the Hebrew language has very few adjectives and so adjectival phrases beginning 'son of' with the appropriate noun are used instead. Sons of God are therefore 'God-like', and so to be called a 'son of God' is as good as being called perfect. The road to world peace begins with each individual; the more like sons of God we each become the nearer we bring the peace of the whole world.

Let us pray:

O God, who art Peace everlasting, whose chosen reward is the gift of peace, and who has taught us that the peacemakers are thy children: Pour thy peace into the souls of thy servants that they may be enabled to impart to men and nations the peace that surpasses all understanding; through Jesus Christ our Lord. Amen.

Daily Prayer

18

9. The Persecuted

'What credit is there in fortitude when you have done wrong and are beaten for it? But when you have behaved well and suffer for it, your fortitude is a fine thing in the sight of God.' So wrote Saint Peter in his First Letter (1 Pet. 2.19, 20). We all tend to complain loudly at injustice; some even object to justice when they are the recipient of a just punishment. 'It's not fair', is the phrase most widely used, but then the whole of life seems grossly unfair.

HYMN: *Who are these like stars appearing?*

'Blessed are they which are persecuted for righteousness' sake, for theirs is the kingdom of heaven.'

There was a time when men thought that goodness was rewarded by prosperity during one's life-time and that the poor and sick were in that state because of sins they had committed. One of the earliest challenges to this line of thought is found in the Book of Job where all sorts of unpleasant things happen to a man who is described as being perfectly good. The book goes some way towards suggesting that there must be some sort of life after death so that the good can be rewarded and the evil punished. The Greek philosopher, Plato, describes a perfectly good man as one who is continually falsely accused of wrong-doing and despite this he does not retaliate in any way. Thus persecution may be defined as 'thoroughly undeserved suffering deliberately inflicted by men upon their fellow human beings'.

In its early days the Christian Church suffered a great deal through persecution. Never, in those days, did Christians fight back; in fact their passive resistance seemed to annoy the persecutors so much that they devised yet more horrible tortures. Persecution is in fact a compliment. Agree with everybody, express no opinion of your own, never make a stand about something you feel to be right you will never be persecuted; but nobody will take any notice of you either. It was because the Christians of the first three centuries AD would not, even for a minute, recognise the Roman Emperor as a god but remained loyal to Christ that they suffered. Men and woman have witnessed for Christ with their lives in other centuries too. There is less persecution of any sort today than some centuries have witnessed; but maybe there are fewer people who are prepared to die for what they believe in. Tolerance is a fine thing . . . indifference is not. Jesus said 'If anyone wishes to be a follower of mine . . . he must take up his cross and come with me.' This does not mean Christians have to provoke others to kill them; it means that a Christian must always be prepared, if necessary, to die rather than to deny Christ; in those circumstances of course you'll not deserve to die, but neither did Jesus deserve to die. To be persecuted is to be complimented as a real Christian and share in the suffering of Our Lord Jesus Christ.

Let us pray:

We humbly beseech thee, O Father, mercifully to look upon our infirmities; and for the glory of thy Name turn from us all those evils which we most righteously have deserved; and grant that in all our troubles we may put our whole trust and confidence in thy mercy, and evermore serve thee in pureness and holiness of living, to thy honour and glory; through our only Mediator and Advocate, Jesus Christ our Lord. Amen.

ARCHBISHOP CRANMER (martyred 1556)

FEASTS AND FASTS

1. All Saints and All Souls

R.I.P., letters we see cut into many a tomb-stone. Fortunately, for most of us the English translation of the original Latin, *Requiescat in pace*, uses the same initial letters as 'Rest in peace'. Many Christians will say that it is wrong to pray for the dead and after all R.I.P. is a prayer; it asks that the dead person may rest in peace, and who else can arrange that but God. I do not think that death ends our obligations to love others so if somebody for whom we prayed when they were alive dies we should continue to remember them in our prayers after their death. Naturally we cannot pray for specific needs of our dead friends because we do not know what they are, though we can ask God to have mercy upon them, and hope that they are resting in peace.

HYMN: *For all the Saints.*

Besides saints who have special 'days' of their own in the Christian year there is one day, 1 November, when the Church remembers all its heroes who do not have a special day. A few have names we know and stories we can hear but many, many, more are entirely unknown to us. On this day we can also remember and rejoice about the good lives they lived. But we all know that some of 'the departed' were far from faithful; every age has had its share of thieves and murderers, cheats and liars. It is these people and the millions of ordinary folk, neither good nor bad, who are remembered on All Souls Day, 1 November. What can we say of these people? The Latin proverb '*Nihil de mortuus nisi bonum*' (Never speak ill of the dead) prevents us from saying

'Thank heavens that rotten blighter is dead and gone. May he rot in hell!' No, we can't say that!

Of the people we consider to have been bad lots here on earth we, as Christians, must hope and pray that they have done some good things about which we have never heard and that God will have mercy upon them. It is about people like this that we should feel sad when they die. The sorrow we feel at the death of a good person is a selfish sorrow that we shall no more derive pleasure from his company. When John and Robert Kennedy were killed, when Martin Luther King was killed it was the world as a whole which was poorer not these three good men who will surely rest in peace.

Let us pray:

O God of Heaven and Earth, we ask you to look with mercy upon all those people we know who have died. We remember relations who have died . . . for some it will be mother or father, for some grandparents, for others aunts and uncles. We also remember friends who we knew well who have now died.[1]

May God have mercy upon the souls of all who have died, the faithful and the not so faithful. This we ask in the name of Jesus Christ our Lord. Amen.

[1] When this prayer was written a member of staff had died and a pupil had been killed during the previous school year; they were remembered by name here.

2. Christmas

Preparations for Christmas are now well under way. Hundreds of pounds have been spent on cards and paper chains. Plans for enormous feasts and extended drinking sessions have been laid. Everything is *planned* and *prepared* so that Christmas will be a great success. The period before Christmas is called Advent; a time of preparation. But I want us to consider two rather different aspects of preparation for Christmas. First of all the Divine preparation for the first Christmas. Second, what preparation we ought to make for Christ's Second Coming.

HYMN: *Hark the glad sound! the Saviour comes.*

How odd
  Of God
    To Choose
      The Jews—So wrote E. N. Ewer.
How odd indeed! How odd to chose that particular moment in time to send his son to earth. But the Jews were far and away the most advanced religious thinkers of their time. Western Europeans were then dancing in woad; the Americans were non-existent; the Greeks had gone up a philosophical blind alley. So it had to be among the Jews. Why not five centuries earlier when Isaiah and the rest could have been alive to see the fulfilment of their prophecies? Why not twenty centuries later when mankind's material well-being was more carefully attended?

The time chosen was just when a world-wide movement had become feasible. The Roman Empire with its ultra-efficient communication system meant that it was possible for ideas to spread beyond the borders of the thinkers' native land. Also in the history of the development of man's ideas about God the time was ripe for a new step forward. Men were ready to entertain the concept of a God of Love. So fundamental and revolutionary was this teaching of Christ that God is love and that men should love their neighbours as themselves that even in nearly twenty centuries we have barely grasped the idea; let alone put it into practice!

This leads me to my second point, that is the Second Coming of Christ. Unlike the members of some religious denominations I am not prepared to act the prophet and name a year. But I am certain that the world will end sooner or later. It may either be *sooner* through a devastating atomic war which will destroy all life on this planet or *later* when knowledge and acceptance of Jesus Christ and a hundred per cent practice of his teaching has become universal. As I say sooner, perhaps sooner than we think, or later, so much later that two thousand years will seem like five minutes by comparison.

In any event we can and ought to prepare ourselves so that whenever the world may end we can justify our having been granted the privilege of a human life with all its opportunities and responsibilities.

Let us pray:

O Christ, most pure and merciful and just, who came into our darkness to be our Saviour: Make us at all times and in all things to love and do only that which will appear merciful, just and pure in the bright light of thy coming again to be our judge, to Jesus who lives and reigns in the glory of the Eternal Trinity, world without end. Amen

E. MILNER WHITE: *Daily Prayer*

3. Epiphany

HYMN: *As with gladness men of old.*

'We three Kings of Orien tar; one in a taxi, one in a car, one on a scooter blowing his hooter . . . ', and so on.

This does remind us of a couple of things about the Kings or Wise Men and ourselves. First of all their method of travel was primitive; they journeyed to Bethlehem by camel. It took them a long time to get from their own country. When they got there all they found was a baby not in the Royal Palace but in a pretty poor district in the suburbs of Jerusalem.

Many of us claim to be Christians and would be most offended if somebody said we were not. But let us compare ourselves with the Kings. First we have motorised transport; they had only camels. They used what they had to go to see the Christ child. How many people today use their means of transport to take them to Church? Through their studies the Kings were sure something wonderful was about to take place. They probably devoted a couple of years of their lives to the pursuit of their idea. Do we show such tenacity of purpose today in the pursuit of an ideal?

All they found was a baby. They might have been tempted to pack up and go home and say 'We made a mistake.' But no; they offered their gifts, gold representing kingship, frankincense representing divinity and myrrh foreshadowing suffering and death. The object of their adoration was a baby. We know about what happened when that baby grew up; we know about his teaching, about his crucifixion, his resurrection and ascension. Do we offer any gifts? Not necessarily of money, but of worship, of time spent in prayer. Are we prepared to allow ourselves to be called Christians just so long as it costs us nothing but give up when it becomes difficult to say 'Yes, I believe in God and in Jesus Christ; Yes I say my prayers; Yes I go to church'? When it becomes difficult to say that sort of thing, do we just go red and avoid answering, do we say 'Oh, no, I think it's all a lot of rot.'?

Many people have just not got enough courage to say they practise Christianity in front of the disbelieving crowd.

In many respects we are twenty centuries in advance of the Kings, but in the matter of faith, devotion, tenacity of purpose, and striving after an ideal we are often twenty centuries behind.

Let us pray:

Almighty and everlasting God, who hast made known the Incarnation of thy dear Son by the testimony of a glorious star, which when the wise men beheld, they adored thy majesty with gifts: Grant that the bright shining of thy truth may lead us always to lay the gifts of our obedience and love at thy feet; through the same thy Son Jesus Christ our Lord. Amen.

E. MILNER-WHITE, (adapted from
'Gelasian Sacramentary'): *Daily Prayer*

4. The Conversion of Saint Paul

Two common features of any religion are miracles and conversions. It is not so much the fact that these take place as the speed at which they happen. We accept that people can recover from an illness but when it happens in an instant we are suspicious. We accept that a man may change his mind about something but we expect this to happen over a period of time and are suspicious if he turns around very suddenly. It is this turning around, conversion or *volte face* idea we are to examine this morning.

HYMN: *Breathe on me breath of God.*

In Hebrew the word *ruah* means 'breath, wind, and spirit'. The hymn we have just sung involves this rather complicated play on words. 'Breathe on me breath of God' could be translated 'Dear God, please may I be influenced by your holy spirit in all that I do so that I can be more like you.'

On the first Whit-Sunday, the fiftieth day after Easter Day, the first disciples were converted. The experience was so strange that it was difficult to describe; however Luke speaks of a 'rushing mighty wind' *ruah* and tongues of fire settling on the heads of the twelve men. Odd. . . . yes, but what an effect it had upon them. Before this event they were in hiding, concealing their identity and not breathing a word to a soul about Christ and his Resurrection. After this event they accused the Jewish leaders of murdering the Son of God and proclaimed all they knew of Jesus in the most public places without the least concern for their personal safety.

Only a few years later one Saul of Tarsus, the most vigorous hater of Christians, was dramatically converted on the road to

Damascus and became *Saint* Paul, one of the greatest Christian missionaries.

Listen to saint Paul's own description of his conversion:

'I myself once thought it my duty to work actively against the name of Jesus of Nazareth; and I did so in Jerusalem. It was I who imprisoned many of God's people by authority obtained from the chief priests; and when they were condemned to death, my vote was cast against them. In all the synagogues I tried by repeated punishment to make them renounce their faith; indeed my fury rose to such a pitch that I extended my persecution to foreign cities.

'On one such occasion I was travelling to Damascus with authority and commission from the chief priests; and as I was on my way, Your Majesty, in the middle of the day I saw a light from the sky, more brilliant than the sun, shining all around me and my travelling-companions. We all fell to the ground, and then I heard a voice saying to me in the Jewish language, 'Saul, Saul, why do you persecute me? It is hard for you, this kicking against the goad.' I said, 'Tell me, Lord, who are you'; and the Lord replied, 'I am Jesus, whom you are persecuting. But now, rise to your feet and stand upright. I have appeared to you for a purpose: to appoint you my servant and witness, to testify both to what you have seen and to what you shall yet see of me.'

Acts 26.9–17

In the eighteenth century John Wesley, the founder of the Methodist Church, felt his 'heart strangely warmed' which he said converted him. There are people today who have 'religious experiences' which they find hard to describe to others but are luminously clear to them and to those who have met the persons concerned both before and after their conversion.

The important thing to remember with Saint Paul, John Wesley and all others who claim to have been converted is that the actual experience, though dramatic in itself, is only the beginning. The test of a conversion is the life led by the converted afterwards. Saint Paul and John Wesley are good examples. They both spent every minute of their post-conversion lives working for Christ.

Every man who becomes a priest or minister prays that he might be indwelt by the Holy Spirit and be enabled to devote the whole of his life to God.

Let us pray:

Almighty God, who dost send thy messengers to prepare the way before thee: endue with the power of the Holy Ghost all who go forth to preach and speak in thy Name. Touch their hearts; enlighten their minds; cleanse and instruct their lips; give them a clear vision of thy will and purpose for the whole world, and through their voice do thou call back thy Church to simpler discipleship, readier obedience, and more loving service; through thy Son, Jesus Christ our Lord. Amen.

Communion with God

5. The Beginning of Lent

'Pancake Day', or to use the correct phrase 'Shrove' Tuesday. The Oxford Dictionary says 'shrive (shrove, shriven) archaic, hear confession of and assign penance to; from the Old English "to write" '. Ash Wednesday was so called because those who had confessed and been given a penance (that is, something to do to show they were really sorry for their misdeeds, not a punishment because it was undertaken voluntarily) those people, in mediaeval days wore sack-cloth and put ashes on their heads. People who have seen the film *Becket* will remember that King Henry II dressed like this after Thomas Becket had been murdered.

Ash Wednesday marks the beginning of the season of Lent in the Church's Year. This is to remind people of the forty days Jesus spent in fasting and prayer before he began preaching and healing. The word 'Lent' comes from another Old English word meaning 'to get longer', and is probably connected with the lengthening of the period of daylight which occurs in Spring.

HYMN: *O for a closer walk with God.*

Now we have defined terms, let us see what Lent ought to mean to us, if anything. Look again at verse three of the hymn. Why is it good for people to give up things for Lent; to give up smoking, sweets, drinking, the cinema, television, pop records? There are two reasons.

First, they make sure their mind is the master of their own bodies, so that drinking, sweet-eating and smoking do not become addictions. To prove to themselves they can do without various luxuries. This does help people to form strong characters because they come to know that if they want to do a thing they have the mental and spiritual strength to do so.

Second, they sacrifice something they enjoy and devote the money and time they save to helping others. Instead of watching the local team play football you offer to do odd jobs for elderly people in your area. Instead of buying the latest pop record you do the shopping for some old or poor person and with the price of the record buy a small present for the person. Every time you have the urge to buy a packet of cigarettes, drop half-a-crown in a collection box of some charity.

We can all do something. Let us now resolve to do some good for others by giving up something we enjoy from today until the end of term; to remind us of the debt we owe Jesus Christ who gave up so much for us.

Let us now pray two prayers for the beginning of Lent:

> O Lord God, who knowest that we have many temptations to conquer, many evils to shun, many difficulties to overcome, and as many opportunities of good: So order our goings that we may observe in all things the perfect rule of Christ, and set ourselves to serve thee first, others next, and ourselves last; through the same Jesus Christ our Lord. Amen.
>
> E. MILNER-WHITE: *Daily Prayer*

> O, God, who in thy love hast bestowed upon us gifts such as our fathers never knew nor dreamed of: Mercifully grant that we be not so occupied with material things that we forget the things which are spiritual; lest, having gained the whole world, we lose our own soul; for thy mercy's sake. Amen.
>
> G. W. BRIGGS: *Daily Prayer*

6. Ash Wednesday

HYMN: *Forty days and forty nights*

Let us pray:

> Almighty God, our heavenly Father, who of thy great mercy
> hast promised forgiveness of sins to all them that with
> sincere repentance and true faith turn unto thee, have mercy
> upon us; pardon and deliver us from all our sins; confirm and
> strengthen us in all goodness, and bring us to everlasting life;
> through Jesus Christ our Lord. Amen.
>
> *The Book of Common Prayer*, 1662 (adapted)

Lent is the season of the Church's Year lasting for forty days
before Easter when Christians think of the forty days Christ
spent in the Wilderness fasting and meditating about the way in
which he was going to tackle his life's work.

The word 'fast' for us implies either speed or more rarely we
say something is 'stuck fast' or somebody is 'fast asleep'. But when
Jesus used the word his Jewish hearers immediately thought
of a period of abstinence from food or at least a reduction in
diet. This was not for reasons of physical health but of spiritual
health.

This is what Jesus said:

> 'So too when you fast, do not look gloomy like the hypo-
> crites: they make their faces unsightly so that other people

34

may see that they are fasting. I tell you this: they have their reward already. But when you fast, anoint your head and wash your face, so that men may not see that you are fasting, but only your Father who is in the secret place; and your Father who sees what is secret will give you your reward.'

Matthew 6.16–18

The section this extract comes from deals with almsgiving, prayer and then fasting. These three cover the whole of religion. Almsgiving represents our duty to our neighbour; prayer our duty to God; and fasting our duty to ourselves.

How can fasting help ourselves? It makes sure we have self-control, self-discipline. Nothing spiritually is really gained if everybody comments 'MY! How thin you're looking.' and you say 'Oh yes I know, I'm fasting; it's very hard but I can manage, I think.' This was the mistake of the Pharisees 'I fast twice in the week . . . , and so on. So they did, Mondays and Thursdays; but their motive was wrong.

If we do decide to deny ourselves something by fasting we can also do something about the other two sections of religion. Money saved by giving up sweets or cinema visits can be given to help to feed the starving; time saved by giving up a T.V. programme can be spent by reading from the Bible or a book on a religious subject or by going to a week-night service at a church. Many churches run courses for the Five Weeks of Lent to help people in this way.

If used properly, Lent can be a time when one's own spiritual welfare is enhanced and so good is done to alleviate a small part of the vast suffering of the world.

Let us pray:

May the Lord forgive what we have been; sanctify what we are; and order what we shall be; for his Name's sake. Amen.

A Book of Prayers for Schools

THE MESSIAH

This section contains six Assemblies suitable for use during Lent. The thoughts centre around six extracts from Handel's *Messiah*. It is suggested that as much of the extract as is convenient should be 'taped'.

The six subjects dealt with are as follows:

(i) Comfort ye
(ii) The Darkness
(iii) Rejection
(iv) Crucifixion
(v) The Resurrection of Jesus
(vi) General Resurrection

7. The Messiah (i) Comfort ye

In every religion music forms an important part in the worship of the people. Music sometimes stands on its own, but sometimes re-expresses ideas which have been written in word form. Shaw's *Pygmalion* was highly regarded as a play but then Messrs. Lerner and Lowe put it to music and called it *My Fair Lady*. *Romeo and Juliet* is brought up to date, set to music and re-named *West Side Story*. Handel has done the same thing for the life of Jesus Christ as reported in the Gospels; I refer, of course, to *The Messiah*. Today and the next few weeks I'm going to play short extracts from this religious musical. We shall now hear some words of Isaiah which John Baptist quoted with reference to Jesus:

MUSIC: *Recitative: Comfort ye, my people.*

There are two points I want to make about this:
First, John was suggesting that people should repent; religious leaders, priests and ministers ever since have exhorted people to *repent*. But what does 'repent' mean?

(a) To be sorry for what wrong you have done. Some do wrong and don't care; some even want to do wrong. *Be sorry.*
(b) To make amends for the wrong you have done. Return the money or goods stolen; make good the damage done for 'kicks'. *Make amends.*
(c) Promise never to do the wrong again.

Repentance is something more than just being sorry; more than just paying for damage; more than just not repenting the wrong. It is all three of these.

The season of Lent is an excellent time for people to have a really good, long look at themselves, to see how far they fall short of their *own* ideals, let alone the perfection of Jesus Christ. Let us look at ourselves and try and rid ourselves of one or two of our worst faults; nobody can pretend he has no faults, so let us all try.

Let us pray:

Most gracious Almighty God, We confess unto thee, we confess with our whole heart, our neglect and forgetfulness of thy commandments, our wrong doing, speaking and thinking, the hurts we have done to others, and the good we have left undone: O Lord, blot out, we beseech thee, the transgressions that are against us, for thy goodness and thy glory, and for the sake of thy Son our Saviour Jesus Christ. Amen.

Daily Prayer (adapted)

Second, The first words we heard sung were '*Comfort ye, comfort ye*'. Neither Isaiah nor John had in mind the arm-chair, soft cushion, good programme, warm fire sort of comfort. They placed emphasis on the *fort* part of the word. A fort is a strong, safe place. We too can be comforted, or made strong, through prayer and with the help of the Holy Ghost. We need to be comforted in this way to ensure that we fulfil all the parts of our repentance.

Let us pray:

The grace of our Lord Jesus Christ, and the love of God, and the fellowship of the Holy Ghost, be with us all evermore. Amen.

2 Cor. 13

8. The Messiah (ii) The Darkness

HYMN: *Lead us heavenly Father, lead us.*

Have you noticed how in our society different colours become associated with different ideas?

We talk of the *reds* when we mean communists.

We speak of somebody's being *green* with envy.

Old so-and-so is in a *black* mood.

The boy who runs from a fight is *yellow*.

We also tend to think of ignorance and evil being dark or *black* and good and knowledge being light or *white*.

This is what Saint John was talking about in that very difficult first chapter of his Gospel. Jesus is the light which came to shine in our darkness. Christ and knowledge of his ideas are good and so represented by light, which should help man to leave his dark and evil ways.

The extract we are to hear from the Messiah is about these ideas: 'The people that walked in darkness have seen a great light: they that dwell in the land of the shadow of death, on them has the light shined.'

MUSIC: *Air: The people that walked in darkness.*

This means simply that Jesus Christ came to the world to give an example of a perfect human life, to suggest ways in which men could try to follow his example and to give them the power to do so. He used no force, neither physical nor mental, to make people follow him. Any man can refuse to open his eyes and take advantage of the light, but the opportunity for help and guidance in the difficult task of living a reasonably good life is there. We have to choose whether to accept it, or to reject it; the people of Palestine in the time of Christ's life on earth had the choice, and it was a free choice. Some of them chose to reject him and his ideas; what are we going to do?

Let us pray:

O Lord the only wise, the God and Father of all, who hast shown unto man light and darkness, right and wrong, that he may choose freely between them; Grant us both generosity and courage to choose the good and to refuse the evil, that we may be numbered among thy sons in whom thou art well-pleased, and who dwell in thy presence; through Jesus Christ our Lord. Amen.

E. MILNER-WHITE: *Daily Prayer*

9. The Messiah (iii) Rejection

One twentieth-century method of rejecting Christ is by saying 'Ah well, there's another crack-pot. He'll get over it,' The Jews were not apathetic; Jesus had shown them where they had gone wrong; he told them they had turned God's law into a god in its own right, and that in their efforts to obey the letter of the law, they forgot all about the spirit of it. They could not dismiss Jesus as a crank; they had either to prove him to be wrong or to get rid of him. Every attempt using the first method failed so they bullied the Roman governor into condemning him to death on a trumped-up charge of being a danger to the Roman Empire. The weak Pilate gave way to the determined Jews in spite of misgivings.

Handel records this event in *The Messiah*. The words he sets to music are: 'He is despised and rejected of men; a man of sorrows and acquainted with grief: we hid as it were our faces from him.'

MUSIC: *Air: He was despised and rejected.*

Christ suffered the pain of physical torture and the mental pain of being rejected by all, even his closest followers, though they came to regret it later. He warned that all who followed him would be likely to have to bear a certain amount of suffering: 'If any man would come after me, let him deny himself and take up his cross daily and follow me.'

Let those of us who would like to think we were Christians reflect now on how much 'rejection' we are prepared to undergo for the sake of Jesus Christ. We have all failed in some way. There is still time before Easter, still time to sacrifice something for the sake of him who suffered and died for us.

HYMN: *When I survey the wondrous cross.*

Let us pray:

Almighty God, whose beloved Son, for our sake, willingly offered himself to endure the Cross, its agony and its shame: Remove from us all coldness and cowardice of heart, and give us courage to take up our cross and follow him; through the same Jesus Christ our Lord. Amen.

G. W. BRIGGS: *Daily Prayer*

10. The Messiah (iv) Crucifixion

MUSIC: *Chorus: And with his stripes we are healed.*

'He saved others; let him save himself if he be the Christ, the elect of God' (Luke 23.35). 'You who would destroy the Temple of God and in three days build it up again. Save yourself! Come down from the cross' (Mark 15.29f.).

Christ died on the cross on Good Friday. Men and woman over the ages have always been amazed at the thought of a God who died. Why did God allow it? Why does God allow disease, suffering, why does God allow . . . ? The paradox of a dying God is expressed in the hymn we are to sing.

HYMN: *Ride on, ride on in majesty.*

Why *did* Jesus, the only *perfect* man, have to die? Because he was a perfect man. Once a person is born it is absolutely inevitable that he will die sooner or later. Jesus was born and lived a life in every way human; to have dodged death and the suffering that goes with it would have ruined the whole idea of God's living a human life. The account of Jesus' prayers in Gethsemane show that he was tempted to say 'O.K. I've shown them how to live a perfect life; they can take it or leave it. I'm going to leave this earth and rejoin my heavenly father.' However he actually said 'Never-the-less thy will not mine, be done.' So, Jesus had to die.

But why did he have to die such an uncomfortable and slow death? Could he not have died in his sleep one night? NO! The thing man seems to fear most is death; not the fact that one minute he will be alive and the next dead; but the whole business of dying. We, quite rightly, regard suffering and disease as evil. Jesus, the Son of God, was good. The Cross was the ultimate point of conflict between good and evil.

All the forces of evil in many forms tried their strength on the good man, Jesus; the Pharisees were jealous of him; Judas thought he knew best when in fact he did not; Pilate did not have the courage of his convictions, no 'guts' as we might say; the High Priests wanted him dead. All these things brought Jesus to the cross. But there were other forces which tried to break the will of Jesus and goad him into using his divine power to save his own skin; the callousness of the soldiers; the gibes of the by-standers; the pain of the nails; the burning heat of the sun; the look of anguish on his mother's face. Nothing was able to tempt Jesus away from being a perfect *man* right up to the moment of death. Then, in his own words, it was finished, his mission completed; his life had been that of a perfect man; the forces of evil had done their worst to the extent of destroying his body; death was evil's trump card but Christ remains; there is something beyond death utterly unapproachable by evil. For the Christian death, the ultimate evil, is not the end but merely the door to the next stage of man's existence.

Let us pray:

O Lord Jesus Christ, who for the redemption of mankind died upon the Cross, that the whole world which lay in darkness might be enlightened: we beseech thee pour such light into our souls and bodies that we may be enabled to attain to that light which is eternal, and through the merits of thy passion may after death joyfully enter within the gates of paradise, who, with the Father and the Holy Ghost, livest and reignest, one God, world without end. Amen.

A Chain of Prayer Across the Ages

11. The Messiah
(v) The Resurrection of Jesus

You might think the Christian Church a rather blood-thirsty lot, their symbol is a cross, and death by crucifixion was very unpleasant—a combination of starvation, exposure and, if you were unlucky enough to be nailed rather than tied, loss of blood. Then nearly all saints are remembered on the anniversary of their death and fifty per cent of the time it was a violent death; burnt at the stake, gored by bulls, mauled by lions, hacked to death by gladiators, riddled with arrows . . .

Death is a necessary step before Resurrection and Resurrection is of great importance to Christianity. There is *the* Resurrection of Jesus and then the idea of a general resurrection of all people. It is with the Resurrection of Jesus that we are concerned today.

HYMN: *The strife is o'er the battle done.*

Dozens of books have been written claiming to explain what happened between about noon one Friday and dawn the following Sunday. *The Day Christ Died* by Jim Bishop; *Who Moved the Stone* by Frank Morison; *The Passover Plot* by Hugh Schonfield all discuss the Resurrection of Jesus and have different points of view to put forward. Christianity as a religion (as distinct from being a moral code) depends for its very existence upon the truth of the Resurrection. Those who wish to disprove the Resurrection today accept that Jesus was an ordinary, though an exceptionally good, man. No man could ever survive crucifixion and so a theory which suggests Jesus was spoofing, pretending to be dead and in the tomb, having escaped Houdini-style from his grave clothes, just pushed aside the very heavy stone and simply walked out, seems more incredible than the traditional account.

45

If one ignores the written evidence of the Four Gospels, which are, of course, biased, there is still quite an amount of evidence which can be amassed in favour of the Resurrection.

First, the Apostles and the early church as a whole made the Resurrection the central point of all their preaching, because many of them had actually seen the risen Christ. Thomas who doubted the Resurrection exclaimed 'My Lord and my God' when he actually saw Jesus; two disciples ran seven miles back to Jerusalem from the village of Emmaus when they realised they had been talking with Jesus; it was an encounter with Jesus Christ which changed Saul of Tarsus, enemy of the church, into the greatest Christian missionary.

Second, nobody ever wanted to disprove the Resurrection more than the Jewish leaders of the day and they could not.

Third, there has never been any alternative story. If the Apostles made it all up it is unlikely that the truth would not have reached the surface.

Fourth, friends and admirers of any dead hero always like to visit his burial place to pay their 'last respects'; many will remember how thousands of people flocked to see Sir Winston Churchill's grave in the months after his funeral. When the women visited the place where Jesus had been buried all they found was an empty tomb. If the body had been moved by some men employed by the High Priest then those men would be able to say where the final resting place of the body of Christ was. If this had been the case Mary and the other women would have made enquiries so they could give Jesus a 'decent burial'.

Turning to the Gospels, everything in Jesus' life and in his recorded sayings fits in exactly with the actual events they record. The consistency is strong evidence against fabrication. Men of the twentieth century are not the first to query the Resurrection, but the Gospel accounts remain unshaken.

Let us conclude by hearing another extract from Handel's Messiah . . . 'I know that my Redeemer liveth'.

12. The Messiah
(vi) General Resurrection

'I believe in the resurrection of the body.'

Part of the joy of Easter is the assurance that resurrection is part of our future as it was realised in *The* Resurrection of Jesus Christ.

HYMN: *Jesus lives!*

'May we go where he is gone' we have just sung . . .well what evidence is produced to back up this comforting promise?

Every religion from the most primitive to the most sophisticated has ideas about the future of a man after his body has ceased to function. Most people have heard of the 'transmigration of souls' theory. This is the suggestion that when we die our souls or inmost selves immediately enter new creatures then being born. What these creatures are depends upon how 'naughty' we were in our lives just ended. If we were good then we are likely to find ourselves in a wealthy family endowed with physical beauty and intellectual gifts. If we had been not so good we might be a sickly pig in a dingy sty. To many this is not satisfactory because the individual is not seen to be very important. Which is really you? What you *were* last time? Or what you *will be* next time? Further, where do the original souls come from and what provision is there for making new souls to occupy the constantly increasing number of bodies being born?

At the other end of the scale the Christian has to find an answer to such questions as 'If there is a resurrection of everyone's body, where is there a place large enough to contain them? How can they be fed? Do resurrected people marry?' Both Jesus and some of his Apostles, notably Saint Paul, had to deal with such questions as these. Both said that the type of body we are to expect after death will be very different from the one we're trying to get used to now. But, both were quite definite in saying that there will be *a* resurrection for everyone, a resurrection of the body.

None of this is much help to the non-Christian but if you believe in Jesus Christ then you will accept his promises as true—'I shall come again and receive you to myself so that where I am you may be also.' Saint Paul points out that any future body we may have will be as different from our present body as birds differ from fish.

If there is no resurrection for us then death wins; when we die that is the end. But Christianity offers hope, through Christ. Again quoting Saint Paul, Death is swallowed up in victory... For the trumpet will sound and the dead will rise immortal.

MUSIC: *The trumpet will sound.*

13. Easter

HYMN: *There is a green hill far away.*

Do you ever buy Easter cards? Even if you do not no doubt you have seen a selection in the shops. Fluffy day-old chicks stand proudly by the shell from which they have just emerged, buds of all colours and Spring flowers of all varieties ooze sentiment and the words gush out Easter greetings. For weeks now Easter eggs have been on sale. But what has this to do with Easter? If you look hard enough you may find an effeminate-looking half-ghost draped with a sheet gazing mournfully at you out of a bunch of primroses. Is this really what Easter is about?

There are several very different ideas all of value connected with Easter. In about 1400 BC a small group of Hebrew slaves left their Egyptian masters to search for the Promised Land. The Pharaoh of the day was reluctant to let them go but eventually they made it after a mysterious disease had killed all the eldest children of the Egyptians but had done no harm to any of the Hebrews. They claimed that the Angel of Death had passed over them. Hence the word *Passover*. Jews celebrate this occasion annually with the killing and eating of a lamb as they have done for three and a half thousand years.

The events of the first Easter occurred during the celebration of the Jewish Passover. Soon symbolism likening Jesus to the lamb which was sacrificed by the Jews crept into Christian thought. When Christianity came to Southern England with Saint Augustine he modified a celebration of the Ancient Britons to include the Christian Easter. This celebration was in honour of the goddess Eostre who was the goddess of fertility, hence the reference to eggs and skipping lambs and budding flowers. Twentieth-century Easter, then, is a combination of all these elements.

First, it is the pagan Spring festival with its emphasis on fertility, of animals and crops.

Second it is a Jewish thanksgiving for deliverance.

Third, it is the central Christian time of rejoicing for the life of Christ and his resurrection.

All three are connected with life and show man's progress over the years. 'Eostre' reminds us of the fact of life in animals and plants and the necessity of its continuation—'Passover' reminds us of our heritage as a people, and our life as human beings. 'Easter' tells us of life everlasting—of life beyond the earthly grave. Each part can have meaning in itself but only by considering all three aspects can Easter be enjoyed to the fullest extent.

Let us pray:

O God, the living God, who hast given unto us a living hope by the resurrection of Jesus Christ from the dead: Grant that we, being risen with him, may seek the things which are above, and be made partakers of the life eternal; through the same Jesus Christ our Lord. Amen.

Daily Prayer

14. Ascension Day

There comes a time in the life of everybody when he has to stand on his own two feet and take full responsibility for his own actions and act and exist entirely independently of parents and teachers and other people whose aim it is to guide, counsel, support and protect the young. Some are no doubt muttering 'Roll on that day', others may not be so keen to be out on their own, nevertheless it is inevitable that it will happen. A similar process of emancipation took place with regard to the Apostles and Jesus. Eventually Jesus left them on their own: this happened at the Ascension which is to be commemorated today.

HYMN: *Rejoice the Lord is king.*

Saint Luke concludes his Gospel with a brief account of the Ascension:

> And he said to them, 'This is what I meant by saying, while I was still with you, that everything written about me in the Law of Moses and in the prophets and psalms was bound to be fulfilled.' Then he opened their minds to understand the scriptures. 'This', he said, 'is what is written: that the Messiah is to suffer death and to rise from the dead on the third day, and that in his name repentance bringing the forgiveness of sins is to be proclaimed to all nations. Begin from Jerusalem: it is you who are the witnesses to all this. And mark this: I am sending upon you my Father's promised gift; so stay here in this city until you are armed with the power from above.'

C

Then he led them out as far as Bethany, and blessed them with uplifted hands; and in the act of blessing he parted from them. And they returned to Jerusalem with great joy, and spent all their time in the temple praising God.

Luke 24.44–53

The Resurrection showed:

First, that Jesus was God, and that evil at its worst was ineffective in its attempts to destroy him.

Second, that death was not the end of everything but the completion of a stage.

Third, that therefore the disciples were wrong in their disillusionment and fear.

The Ascension was necessary to allow the Apostles and disciples to stand on their own feet. If Jesus was not immediately on hand in the flesh with help, they would have to do the work themselves. If one of you were to start painting a picture but the Art Master were to do ninety per cent of the work, although it might be a very good picture he could not have the pleasure of saying 'My, that lad is a good artist' and feel he had taught you well. So the time came when the disciples were on their own; they were not completely deserted as we know. The time will come when you will all be on your own, although you will not be completely deserted because there will still be people you can consult. *Now* it is up to parents and teachers to advise; *later* it will be up to you to seek advice when you need it. During Jesus' earthly life he advised the Apostles; after the Ascension he was, and still is, available to advise when he is sought through prayer. God does not impose his will; we can choose whether or not to ask his advice. Independence, in whatever field, brings responsibility; the greater the freedom, the greater the responsibility.

Let us make the words of the poet John Donne our own as we pray:

'O Lord, never allow us to think we can stand by ourselves, and not need thee.' Amen.

15. Whitsun

Time after time in the New Testament we read such phrases as 'The Holy Spirit came upon them', 'they were filled with the Holy Spirit'. Next Sunday will be Whit-Sunday, the anniversary of the day on which the Apostles received the Holy Spirit.

HYMN: *Spirit of mercy, truth, and love.*

Next Sunday is Whit-Sunday. The date of Easter varies according to the moon over a period of thirty-five days, and Whit-Sunday is exactly fifty days after Easter Sunday; the government has decided that the Bank Holiday normally taken on Whit-Monday will now take place on the last Monday in May, regardless of when the churches celebrate Whitsun. And we will get our half-term break then.

We will deal with four questions concerning the Holy Spirit:

What, or rather who, is this Holy Spirit the early Christians claim to have received? First of all let us remember that Holy Spirit, Holy Ghost, the Comforter, and the Paraclete are all the names of the same person of the Trinity. Father, Son and Holy Spirit are all God. The Trinity is a way of explaining the nature of God and uses the phrase 'three persons in one God' The Holy Spirit is one of those persons.

To whom is he given? He is given to those who love and admire Jesus Christ and who try to put his teaching into practice. The gift is conditional only upon our loving and obeying Jesus. No other stipulation as to age, qualifications, race or colour is made.

Why is he given? He is given to ensure Christs' presence. At the time of the Ascension Jesus said 'I will not leave you comfortless.'

Hence the Holy Spirit is sometimes called the 'comforter'.

What does he do when he has come?

First, 'comfort'—not in the modern sense but rather 'call along-side to help'; to strengthen us in our life and service in the world.

Second, Spirit of Truth is another name given to the Holy Spirit. The source of inspiration, the feeling we have that a certain course of action is right for us, that is the work of the Holy Spirit.

Let us pray:

O God, who art in every place, and every place where thou art is holy ground: Fill our hearts with awe and wonder as we pass along the common ways of life; that in them we may behold thee, and beholding bow down before thy presence; through Jesus Christ our Lord. Amen.

G. W. BRIGGS: *Daily Prayer*

We pray not, O Lord our God, that thou shouldest reveal thyself by outward signs of mighty works, but in the quiet solitude of our inmost heart; not by the thunder and the lightning, but by the still small voice; and when thou speakest, give, we beseech thee, to thy servants the hearing ear, and a heart to obey; through Jesus Christ our Lord. Amen.

G. W. BRIGGS: *Daily Prayer*

THE LORD'S PRAYER

1. 'Our Father'

Whenever somebody begins to talk about prayer sooner or later he will mention the Lord's Prayer. For a few weeks we are to examine in some detail the various petitions of this most famous prayer to see what they really mean. Today the subject is the opening couple of words 'Our Father.'

HYMN: *Dear Lord and Father of mankind, forgive our foolish ways.*

'Our Father'—two simple words which contain a wealth of meaning. This was the prayer that Jesus taught his disciples himself. Jesus always spoke of God as his father. The ideal father is somebody who is always near at hand, somebody who is prepared to listen sympathetically at all times, but he is also somebody who expects obedience from his children. Now we all, immediately we hear the word 'obedience', tend to think of the droopy - moustached - completely - insensitive - Victorian type of father. But when we are talking of an ideal father we are wrong to consider obedience in this light. Obedience need not be exacted through fear, it can be induced through love. The word translated in the Bible 'father' is an Aramaic word which stands half-way in meaning between the child's word 'daddy' and the more formal 'father'. We should remember every time we say 'Our Father', and this applies to all of us, young and old, parents and children, that by using this phrase we acknowledge the relationship of love that exists between ourselves and our God.

God as father is interested in us as individuals. He cares about us. We are free to allow ourselves to be guided by him.

In addition to this relationship between God and us as individuals these opening words have something to tell us about our relationship with the rest of mankind. The first word is *'Our'*, not *'My* father', or 'Aunt Mary's father' or 'the vicar's father' but *'Our* Father'. Those who share a father are brothers and sisters and so in the Lord's Prayer we begin by acknowledging the unity of mankind; class, race, colour, nationality, financial status all melt into the background as Christians join in the 'Great Family Prayer of the Church' taught us by Jesus Christ, beginning 'Our Father. . . .'

Let us pray:

O God that art always a Father at hand and not a Lord far off, that changest not but art the same yesterday, today and for ever: Govern thou the thoughts of our mind, the words of our mouth, the works of our fingers and the desire of our hearts, until thy love and thy likeness be perfected in us; through Jesus Christ our Lord. Amen.

E. MILNER-WHITE: *Daily Prayer*

2. 'Which art in Heaven'

HYMN: *O worship the King*

First of all anybody who knows any English grammar will object that it should be 'who' not 'which art in heaven'. God is a person not a thing. The Archbishop of Canterbury said a while ago that he was going to authorise a number of changes in the wording of the Lord's Prayer and this is one of them. This is the sensible thing to do.

Once we have said the words 'Our Father' we have acknowledged that there is a God, and as human beings we cannot leave it at that but we have to speculate about where God is to be found. The word we use is 'heaven'. Artists who paint their idea of God fill in the background with their idea of heaven, but it is *their* idea both of how God looks and where he is to be found. The artist is limited by space; no matter how hard he tries to avoid it he must limit his representation of God who is infinite and without limit. The aim of most artists is to paint a scene of great beauty thinking of the verse from the psalm which says 'Worship him in the beauty of his holiness.'

Theologians, philosophers, poets and writers also try to describe where and what heaven is. Some make it sound like a six-starred hotel with all 'mod. cons.' others find heaven a source of endless jokes about Saint Peter letting in some people and sending others elsewhere. The truth is that nobody knows what heaven is really like, we can only believe that it exists; we can all have our own ideas about it, but nobody can be dogmatic. The basic Christian teaching is that heaven is complete unity with God and that each person begins to create his own heaven by living in accordance with God's will. The closer he follows the will of God the nearer he reaches heaven; death does not interrupt this progress but merely marks the completion of a stage; a barrier which has to be passed before one can go on to the next stage. For me therefore the clause 'which art in heaven' does not add very much because God is heaven and heaven is God. It is interesting to note that Saint Luke does not record Jesus' mentioning this clause to the Twelve, though Saint Matthew does. When we say these words we remind ourselves that God, and heaven, and life or existence after death are all very closely connected together and all three are connected with each one of us and our own lives.

Let us pray:

Almighty God, in whom we live and move and have our being: give us faith to know that we can no more be removed from thy presence than from our own; and since thou seest every action, hearest all our conversation and knowest all our thoughts, restrain and guide us in all our ways, that we may become completely united with thee; through Jesus Christ, thy Son, our Lord and Saviour. Amen.

Daily Prayer (adapted)

3. 'Hallowed be thy name'

In the first two petitions of the Lord's Prayer we have looked at, we have seen that between God and man there is a close personal relationship, that by the use of the word 'our' all mankind are brothers and sisters equal children of God; that by falling in with God's idea of behaviour we can reach 'heaven'. All this is very cosy; here we are on chatty terms with God feeling sure of our place in life, both now and later. But the next petition, 'Hallowed be thy name', brings us back to reality. God is very hard for us to understand. When we see something perfect we stand back and just look and admire; some men feel this about diamonds, some about a landscape, some about the sea, some a picture or piece of sculpture. 'It's perfect . . . , just perfect', they say. God is absolute perfection. What can one say?

HYMN: *Holy, holy, holy! Lord God Almighty!*

After this I looked, and there before my eyes was a door opened in heaven; and the voice that I had first heard speaking to me like a trumpet said, 'Come up here, and I will show you what must happen hereafter.' At once I was caught up by the Spirit. There in heaven stood a throne, and on the throne sat one whose appearance was like the gleam of jasper and cornelian; and round the throne was a rainbow, bright as an emerald. In a circle about this throne were twenty-four other thrones, and on them sat twenty-four elders, robed in white and wearing crowns of gold. From the throne went out flashes of lightning and peals of thunder. Burning before the throne were seven flaming torches, the seven spirits of God, and in front of it stretched what seemed a sea of glass, like a sheet of ice.

In the centre, round the throne itself, were four living creatures, covered with eyes, in front and behind. The first creature was like a lion, the second like an ox, the third had a human face, the fourth was like an eagle in flight. The four, living creatures, each of them with six wings, had eyes all over, inside and out; and by day and by night without a pause they sang:

'Holy, holy, holy is God the sovereign Lord of all, who was, and is, and is to come!'

Rev. 4.1–8

The author here is hallowing the name of God. He is expressing reverence for everything he knows of God. God is holy, God is perfect. There is so much we do not understand; we tend to be afraid of what we do not understand; we tend to abuse what we fear; but we must expect not to be able to understand God. In his presence we can only stand in awe and say 'Holy, holy, holy!'

Let us pray:
O God, whom no man hath seen nor can see, yet who alone canst give our life its meaning, receive us as we come to render thee homage. We gather here to make humble acknowledgement of thy goodness in adoration and praise, and to lift up our hearts to thee in confession of failure, in petition for forgiveness and help, and in intercession for one another, and for all people everywhere. Amen.

A Book of School Worship

4. 'Thy Kingdom come, thy will be done, on earth as it is in heaven.'

HYMN: *Lead us, heavenly Father, lead us*

Admirers of Frankie Howerd will remember one of his programmes where he related what happened when he was visited by a person he had met on holiday. Frankie had said to this person: 'Do come and stay with me when you next visit London', feeling absolutely certain, and hoping very much, that the person would never come, because he could not stand him. Perhaps you have heard parents and relations say to people they do not know all that well, 'You must come over some evening in the Summer.' You notice they take great care never to fix an actual date and then when you innocently ask, 'When are the Fosdykes coming?' you get the reply 'What, those awful people, never I hope!' So this perhaps the attitude of many people who pray quite merrily 'Thy Kingdom come thy will be done, on earth as it is in heaven' and add mentally or under their breath 'but not yet'? Accuse these people of not being Christians and they will spring to their defence with a list of charities they support, but omitting to say how much they give, and the number of times they attend church; but they do really try to bring about God's Kingdom on earth? Usually the answer is 'No!'.

God's Kingdom is not like the United Kingdom or the Kingdom of the Netherlands which cover a certain number of square miles, but rather it refers to the Kingship or reign of God. A society which acknowledges God and tries to put his laws into practice is the Kingdom of God. There are dozens of parables of Jesus each telling us a little more of the Kingdom of God or the Kingdom of

Heaven. The parable of the mustard seed tells about small beginnings but far-reaching results. The wheat and the tares shows that good and evil exist side by side to be sorted out later. The Kingdom is not to be thought of in material terms, or as a political Kingdom. It is not a great organisation which will impose its own ideas upon people. The Kingdom of God is accepted, or rejected, by individuals. Each person must recognise his own terms, like the man who sold all his property to buy the finest pearl in the world. There may well be personal sacrifices to be made in order to obtain entrance.

Doing the will of God is not a last resort; it ought be mankind's first aim. We have seen that we cannot hope to understand fully the workings of the mind of God. But we must try to see his will for us and then try and do it. Young children have complete trust in their parents. Holding a parent's hand they will happily cross the busiest road. They go to school and return home knowing that the home will still be there with its comforts, food and shelter. This is why we call God 'father' and following Jesus, the Son of God, we must be prepared to say and to mean 'Thy Kingdom come' and 'Thy will be done not mine O Lord.'

Let us pray:

Almighty God, give us grace to be not only hearers but doers of thy holy word, not only to admire but to obey thy doctrine, not only to profess but to practise thy religion, not only to love but to live thy Gospel. So grant that what we learn of thy glory we may receive into our hearts and show forth in our lives. Through Jesus Christ our example and Lord. Amen.

5. 'Give us our daily bread'

In our study of the Lord's Prayer we have reached the petition which says 'Give us our daily bread'. Fairy story addicts will be tempted to compare this statement with that made by a little old man (old men are always 'little' in fairy stories) when he spoke to his magic table using the secret formula of 'Little table, be covered' and without fail a white cloth and the best food and wine always promptly appeared. While we sing the hymn let us try and think what other word could have been put in the place of 'bread', and whether that word would be adequate to express all the ideas contained in the phrase 'daily bread'.

HYMN: *All people that on earth do dwell.*

What basic needs did you think of?

Water, milk, butter, coal, dairy produce, meat, potatoes, electricity, gas, transport, telephones, medicines—the list could continue for a long time. Why do we not pray that we may be provided with all the necessities of life each day as we need them, and, please God, a few luxuries too, if possible? But bread is the most suitable word. The father of a family is often called the bread-winner; but if bread was all that he provided he would not be very popular with his wife and children. Bread itself is basic in the diet of most of the Western world and bread can be used in the wider sense of all the requirements for life. So 'bread' is simultaneously a simple word understood in the literal sense by all and an all-embracing word covering every department of human life.

Now we are clear as to the full meaning of bread here but we must also see that occuring where it does in the Lord's Prayer this petition, 'Give us our daily bread' is not at all the same as 'Little table be covered'. Prayer is never the easy way to get God to do for us what we can well do, and must do, for ourselves. Jesus rejected the temptation to use his undoubted power to turn stones into bread to feed himself and furthermore to attract followers by providing free food. God and man must work in partnership. There is a story of a rural gardener in Somerset who was visited by the Vicar. The Vicar said 'My what a beautiful garden you have. You must feel very thankful to the Lord for his goodness'. The gardener replied, 'Oi don' know about that; thee's should 'ave sid it when Lord 'ad it all to hisself; terrible mess, weeds everywhere.' But what can man do on his own without God? No man has ever made a living, growing thing. Scientists can construct a seed using all the right chemicals in the correct proportions but it will not grow.

To pray for our daily bread is to acknowledge our ultimate dependence on God for everything, to ask for him to continue with his 'share' in the satisfaction of our daily requirements, to pledge ourselves to do our part as well, and, as in the whole of the Lord's Prayer, we pray not as individuals, it is not 'give *me my* daily bread, but as members of the whole community of mankind, so the words are *us* and *ours*.

Let us pray:

Father of mercies, and author of all good, whose providence for thy children never faileth, and whose continual blessings are unnumbered: grant that with content and gratitude we may live in the fellowship of labour and the brotherhood of thy family, enjoying thy bounty with rejoicing hearts; through Jesus Christ our Lord. Amen.

BERNARD SNELL

6. 'Forgive us our trespasses, as we forgive them that trespass against us'

HYMN: *O for a heart to praise my God*

'Trespassers will be prosecuted!' A stern but generally ignored warning having, apparently, doubtful legal significance. Yet we pray to have our trespasses forgiven! The word is used to translate a Greek word for which we have not exact equivalent. *The New English Bible* translation is 'Forgive us the wrong we have done as we have forgiven those who have wronged us.'

There are three points I wish to make about this petition:

First, the prayer was given by Jesus for use by all men, not by notoriously wicked people only. Everybody falls short of perfection every day; some days we do worse than others but always there is room for improvement; something we would not do if we had our time again; something we would not say; something we would not think. So all men need to ask God's forgiveness.

Second, forgive us as we have forgiven. Jesus spoke dozens of parables to illustrate the point that unless man is prepared to forgive his fellows he simply cannot expect God to forgive him. The forgiveness of God and the forgiveness of man are very closely connected, you cannot have one without the other. So the man who forgives his fellows can do God's will without ever acknowledging God and will be treated with mercy by God.

Third, the implications of the word 'as' are far-reaching. If we refuse to forgive our fellow men and persist in praying the Lord's Prayer we are inviting God to be as tough with us as we are with the people with whom we come into contact. I often wonder whether those who do not join in the saying of the Lord's Prayer abstain through mere apathy, or whether having examined the words and considered the meaning find that they dare not pray because they cannot in all conscience say 'Our' Father because they do not accept the brotherhood of man; and that to ask God to forgive their wrongdoings only to the extent that they have forgiven others would only be to ask that they might be severely punished.

Belief in God is not the easy way out because it demands of people a certain standard of behaviour and brings with it a number of duties, or obligations, and responsibilities. Being brought up in a Christian home does not make a person a Christian himself. Christianity has to be accepted or rejected by each person individually.

And so by forgiving others we put ourselves in a position in which we can ask God that we might be forgiven for our short comings. But it is no use adopting the attitude 'Now look here God I forgave so-and-so now you can let me off this or that' because, as in the parable Jesus told, we owe God ten thousand talents, about two million pounds, compared with a few pence that is owed to us. We need to be humble and merely to say we have tried our best to forgive others and trust that God will look with mercy upon us.

Let us pray:

Almighty God, our heavenly Father, who of thy great mercy hast promised forgiveness of sins to all them that with sincere repentance and true faith turn unto thee, have mercy upon us; pardon and deliver us from all our sins; confirm and strengthen us in all goodness, and bring us to everlasting life; through Jesus Christ our Lord. Amen.

The Book of Common Prayer, 1662 (adapted)

7. 'Lead us not into temptation'

I have to admit that Christianity is out of date . . . but in one respect only, and that is in the language it so often uses to express its ideas. Christians are continually plagued with words which require the explanation '. . . in the biblical sense of the word'. For example, 'prevent'; this has nothing to do with stopping but comes from the Latin, meaning 'going before'. This means that before one can hope to understand Christianity one must learn its jargon, or technical language. This morning our thoughts will be about the part of the Lord's Prayer 'Lead us not into temptation', which is not very meaningful to us as it stands.

HYMN: *O help us, Lord! Each hour of need thy heavenly succour give.*

Once again we are stuck with a word in the Greek which is very difficult to put into one convenient English word. The word was translated 'temptation' in 1611. The word *peirazein* in Greek, can be used in many senses:

First, to test a product; as a doctor tests a drug or a builder tries out a new kind of brick.

Second, to test somebody's faith. Genesis records the story of how Abraham was asked by God to sacrifice his son; this proved the extent of Abraham's love for God.

Third, to cross-examine. The Pharisees often tried to test Jesus by careful questioning.

And fourth, to tempt in the way that people are tempted to steal when they see money or goods lying around without an owner to guard or to care about them.

There are ways in which each of these four senses is relevant. *The New English Bible* translates this petition 'Do not bring us to the test.' In one sense this is in the spirit of our first definition. We are all closely concerned with exams, but they need only to be feared and hated by those who have not done well because they have fallen a long way short of what was expected of them. So if God were to judge us now we would fail miserably to measure up to the perfection of Christ; so very naturally we pray that God will not choose to judge us yet. We will never escape being examined but the longer we hope for it to be delayed the more prepared we may become.

In a second sense we hope that God will not ask us to do or to give up something for him which will be very hard for us to do. The classic example was Schweitzer who gave up brilliant futures in music, medicine and theology to work in Africa for God.

Thirdly, we pray that we may not be drawn into heated arguments and say all sorts of things we do not mean under a barage of questions we only half understand. There is a time when even the most intelligent people are right to say 'I don't know why, but that is what I believe to be right; I can't prove it but I firmly believe it is so. And there's an end to it until I've had a chance to think.'

And fourthly, and this is very obvious, we ask that we may have the sense not to stick our necks out unnecessarily. The girl who is trying to slim is stupid to work in a cake shop on Saturday mornings because she is putting temptation in her own way. If you know that you cannot afford a particular thing do not hang round a shop which sells it for hours and hours for you will be tempted to steal. You may not steal, but there is no need for you to be tempted so severely.

'Lead us not into temptation.'

'Do not bring us to the test.'

Whichever translation you prefer to accept, the Christian prayer which the words express is the same; the same today as in

1066 as it will be in 3066; the same in Chinese as in Urdu or French.

So there are four things we have to pray about in connection with temptation or testing: The inevitability of examination of our lives by God; that we may be ready. That the cross we have to carry may not be more difficult than we can bear. That we may not be drawn from our principles by false argument. That we may not make things difficult for ourselves, by our own stupidity.

8. 'But deliver us from evil'

HYMN: *Be thou my guardian and my guide.*

In the hymn we have prayed for protection from Satan, from the tempter, from the snares of hell. In the Lord's Prayer we ask to be delivered from evil or, in accordance with *The New English Bible*, the Evil One. Who or what is this Satan, Devil, or Evil One? In the form of a serpent he tempted Eve, so we are told in Genesis. He also tempted Jesus for forty days in the wilderness. Some people believe in a 'personal devil', that is, a power of evil who organises the evil of the world, some do not accept this 'personal' idea, but either way it is a fact that there is evil in the world. Everything that grows also decays and is subject to disease, in humans and animals that decay and disease causes pain. The earth itself is growing in a way, it is constantly changing and its changes sometimes involve destruction; earthquakes, floods, volcanoes. God is subject to none of these things because he is infinite, he never changes, never grows or shrinks, but always remains the same. So everything except God is potentially evil. Man can also be evil for another reason. He can deliberately choose to cause another man pain or he can do this accidentally, But it is always going on; motor-cars are basically for the good of mankind but men have been killed and injured by them; then there is war . . . , death, injury, disease, hunger. The point is that evil is a part of a world which is constantly changing. But that does not mean there is no God. God has given us freedom of choice; if we cannot do wrong there is no choice. Being forced to vote when only one candidate is allowed to stand does not allow men to make a free choice. We have free choice so that wrong, evil, pain, or whatever you call it, is a possibility. We are all affected by the actions of others and so pain we suffer may be most undeserved.

The question of the existence of God is not answered in any way by reference to the existence of evil. This is all by the way. . ., there is evil in the world and we must face this as a fact.

When we pray 'deliver us from evil' we should not be asking that we might be the sole survivors should we be in a plane-crash, or that even if our whole town is swallowed by an earthquake we escape alive and un-injured these are facts of life; we cannot escape them. But what we can and should most earnestly pray for is that we may be protected from ourselves, or from the Devil working within us, so that we do nothing to increase the amount of evil in the world. There is enough suffering brought about by nature without our harming each other. Do not think that this does not affect you, because it does; it affects all of us. There is rarely a day that passes when anybody can honestly say that he did nothing to hurt anybody either physically, or by words, or by failing to do what he could to help another.

'And if I tempted am to sin
Do thou, O Lord, save my soul from wrong.'
In other words 'Deliver us from evil'.

Let us pray:

O Thou, who hast ordained that our life on this earth shall be a struggle, from the beginning even unto the end, so guide and order that struggle, we beseech thee, that what is good in us may prevail over what is evil; that everything may be brought into harmony, and that God may be all in all; grant this through Jesus Christ our Lord. Amen.

WILLIAM KNIGHT: *A Book of Prayers for Schools*

9. 'For thine is the Kingdom'

'Thine, O Lord, is the greatness, and the power, and the glory, and the victory, and the majesty: for all that is in the heaven and the earth is thine; thine is the kingdom, O Lord, and thou art exalted as head above all.' This is a short hymn of praise written by King David in about 1000 BC. In its contracted form this was added to the Lord's Prayer in about AD 100 'For thine is the kingdom, the power, and the glory for ever and ever.'

After praying about temptation and evil it is a relief to be cheerful and to praise God, and so the addition was appropriate. Let us pray:

O Almighty God, without beginning and without end, the Lord of thine own works: We praise and bless thee that thou gavest a beginning to time, and to the world in time, and to mankind in the world; and beseech thee so to dispose all men and all things that they may be gathered up in thee and thine endless heaven; through him who is the first and the last, thine everlasting Word, our Saviour Jesus Christ. Amen.

G. W. BRIGGS: *Daily Prayer*

HYMN: *Songs of praise the angels sang.*

'Thine is the kingdom', as before, 'kingdom' is not an area of land but we acknowledge God to be King and pledge our obedience and allegiance to him. 'The power'—the Greek word for this is *dunamis* from which we get dynamic. The prayer ends with a statement that we know God has heard and will act as he deems fit. It is an act of faith, an expression of confidence in God. 'The glory'—

74

glory is a word which can only be adequately used of God. It is an attempt to express the idea that we are aware of our smallness in every way when compared with God. 'For ever and ever'—God by the very definition of the word must be infinite, and lasting for ever and ever, so this merely states the obvious. 'Amen' —this word means 'So be it', or 'O.K.'—to use the modern idiom. The person saying the prayer concludes and those listening wish to be associated with the ideas they have heard expressed. 'Amen' is the conventional word to use in this case. In some churches you get less conventional cries, which often seem more genuine—the 'Halleluiah' and 'Praise the Lord' one associates with the Negroes of the Southern States.

Our school assemblies, time and oraganisation do not allow all that many people to take a very active part in the service. The words of hymns often leave a lot to be desired but one does feel that one has a part in the service if one sings. The 'Amen' at the end or the prayer is the outward demonstration that one has made the prayer one's own. I like to attend the services of Christian churches other than my own; but I always make it a rule to make myself a *partaker* in that service and not a *spectator*, I do not always succeed but I try. If you are a spectator and not a partaker you miss something. One can also distinguish between *praying* a prayer and *speaking* a prayer. When you *pray* it you take the words and make them your own with every ounce of sincerity you possess. It is said of many activities that you only get out what you put in; this is especially true of worship.

If you put nothing in it becomes a meaningless mumbo-jumbo, but if you really become a partaker it becomes a worthwhile and spiritually refreshing experience.

Let us pray:

O thou who dwellest in every humble heart, and dost consecrate it for thy sanctuary: Hallow, we pray thee, our hearts within us, that they may be houses of prayer, the dwelling-places of thy Spirit, wherein thou dost reveal thy holy mysteries; through Jesus Christ our Lord. Amen.

JEREMY TAYLOR (adapted)

PARABLES

1. Be Prepared

The Scouts' motto is 'Be Prepared'; a firm manufacturing torch batteries makes much of its trade-mark *Ever-ready*. Our hymn this morning has a similar theme as it applies to Christianity.

HYMN: *Ye servants of the Lord, each in his office wait.*

Today about seventy per cent of the population claim to be middle-class. In Palestine at the time of Jesus there was no middle-class, there were the rich and the poor, the servants and the masters. In the parables I am going to read the original hearers would have found it easy to identify themselves with one or other of the characters.

'Be ready for action, with belts fastened and lamps alight. Be like men who wait for their master's return from a wedding-party, ready to let him in the moment he arrives and knocks. Happy are those servants whom the master finds on the alert when he comes. I tell you this: he will buckle his belt, seat them at table, and come and wait on them. Even if it is the middle of the night or before dawn when he comes, happy they if he finds them alert. And remember, if the householder had known what time the burglar was coming he would not have let his house be broken into. Hold yourselves ready, then, because the Son of Man is coming at the time you least expect him.'   *Luke 12.35–40*

Wedding-parties were occasions for about as much eating and drinking then as now and went on far into the night. Nobody who employed a servant would be pleased to discover him asleep when he ought to be prepared to do his duty. The message Jesus wants to get across here is that if we are ready to do the will of God there is no telling what pleasant surprises lie in store for us. Imagine the servants being waited on by their master. What an honour for them! Less remote from our day is the second illustration about the burglar. This, incidentally, is a good example of the dry sense of humour of Jesus. He was a man who made the sort of joke that people smile at rather than roar their heads off. Who is going to let their house be burgled if the thief has been kind enough to let the owner know when he proposes to break in?

Both these short parables have the same meaning but two distinct applications. 'Be prepared' is the meaning of both, but when Jesus spoke them the situation was vastly different from today. The Son of God was there on earth. The way he was treated by those who ought to have known better indicates that they had been caught off-guard; or to make an analogy of the parable, the Jewish leaders represented by the servants were asleep when the master of the household, Jesus the Christ, arrived and were not ready to greet him. And in the second parable the householder, again representing the Jewish nation as a whole, had been warned, through the prophets, of the time that the thief, Jesus the Messiah, was due and yet took no action.

Our situation is more generalised, Jesus promised, and the Church constantly teaches, that the world will come to an end with the return of Christ to judge the world. We must be spiritually prepared . . . now. It is no good saying "I haven't time now to do things for others or to say my prayers, I'll do that later.' Later may never come, you may die before you get round to spiritual things. Let us pray:

Make us, we beseech thee, O Lord, watchful and heedful in awaiting the coming of thy Son Christ our Lord; that when he shall stand at the door and knock, he may find us, not sleeping in carelessness and sin, but awake and rejoicing in his praises; through the same Jesus Christ our Lord. Amen.

E. MILNER-WHITE (adapted from 'Gelasian Sacramentary'): *Daily Prayer*

2. Excuses

HYMN: *How sweet the name of Jesus sounds.*

All of us are experts on the subject of excuses, some on the aspect of trying them on, some in distinguishing the genuine from the false. Everybody makes excuses; Jesus knew this too and told the following parable on the subject.

One of the company, after hearing all this, said to him, 'Happy the man who shall sit at the feast in the kingdom of God!' Jesus answered , 'A man was giving a big dinner party and had sent out many invitations. At dinner-time he sent his servant with a message for his guests, "Please come, everything is now ready." They began one and all to excuse themselves. The first said, "I have bought a piece of land, and I must go and look over it; please accept my apologies." The second said, "I have bought five yoke of oxen, and I am on my way to try them out; please accept my apologies." The next said, "I have just got married and for that reason I cannot come." When the servant came back he reported this to his master. The master of the house was angry and said to him, "Go out quickly into the streets and alleys of the town, and bring me in the poor, the crippled, the blind, and the lame." The servant said, "Sir, your orders have been carried out and there is still room." The master replied, "Go out on to the highways and along the hedgerows and make them come in; I want my house to be full. I tell you that not one of those who were invited shall taste my banquet." '   *Luke 14.15–24*

Now are these excuses valid?

One bought land. Who would buy some land without looking at it? Another bought oxen. Who today would buy a tractor or a car without trying it out? And the third had just got married. There are many jokes about marriage but it should not normally prevent a man from doing what he really believes to be right.

The excuses then are a bit thin. But what were they missing? Jesus is referring to the Kingdon of God, or rather to people doing the will of God. It seemed obvious at the time of Jesus that God would look to the Pharisees and other leading Jews to do his will. They *had* their opportunity, the invitation of the parable refers to this, they refused and so the doors were thrown open to others, any who are willing to listen to the voice of God.

What are the reasons or excuses we offer for not doing the will of God or for not going to church. Are they substantial or thin, weak excuses like those in the parable? An English proverb states that 'Where there's a will there's a way.' This applies to religion perhaps more than to anything else; one can, and many do, get by in life without going to church and without trying to put into practice the teaching of Christianity, but there seems to me to be a whole dimension of life which is ignored by these people; an invitation from God which is refused. In a quiet moment today examine your reasons for not going to church last Sunday or for not doing somebody a good turn, and see if your reasons are really reasons or only just weak excuses

Let us pray:

O Christ, most pure and merciful and just, who came into our darkness to be our Saviour: Make us at all times and in all things to love and do only that which will appear merciful, just and pure in the bright light of thy coming again to be our judge; to Jesus who lives and reigns in the glory of the eternal Trinity, world without end. Amen.

E. MILNER-WHITE: *Daily Prayer*

3. Forgiveness

A character in one of Shaw's plays was always saying very loudly 'I never apologise', and a Shakespearian character said 'Words, words, mere words no matter from the heart.' These two quotations are typical of two common attitudes towards being sorry, the one is never sorry and is proud of it, the other will say anything which is expedient believing that words do not matter at all. Into which category do you come?

The author of our hymn is in a third category; he is sorry for all his shortcomings. He speaks of 'contrite anguish sore' in other words he is very sorry indeed.

HYMN: *O help us, Lord! Each hour of need.*

When speaking of God Jesus usually dwelt upon his love for man and this leads some to think of God as an 'old softie' like a benevolent grandfather who is not capable of being really cross and will 'let you off' no matter what you have done. Actually some of the sternest and potentially frightening teaching of Jesus concerns the forgiveness of God.

'The kingdom of Heaven should be thought of in this way: There was once a king who decided to settle accounts with the men who served him. At the outset there appeared before him a man whose debt ran into millions. Since he had no means of paying, his master ordered him to be sold to meet the debt, with his wife, his children, and everything he had. The man fell prostrate at his master's feet. 'Be patient with me,' he said, "and I will pay in full"; and the master was so moved

83

D

with pity that he let the man go and remitted the debt. But no sooner had the man gone out than he met a fellow-servant who owed him a few pounds; and catching hold of him he gripped him by the throat and said, "Pay me what you owe." The man fell at his fellow-servant's feet, and begged him, "Be patient with me, and I will pay you"; but he refused, and had him jailed until he should pay the debt. The other servants were deeply distressed when they saw what had happened, and they went to their master and told him the whole story. He accordingly sent for the man. "You scoundrel!" he said to him; "I remitted the whole of your debt when you appealed to me; were you not bound to show your fellow-servant the same pity as I showed to you?" And so angry was the master that he condemned the man to torture until he should pay the debt in full. And that is how my heavenly Father will deal with you, unless you each forgive your brother from your hearts.' *Matthew 18.23-35*

Many Christian prayers are requests for forgiveness and rightly so because we all fall a long, long way short of perfection every day. But the important thing is to make sure we have been as forgiving to others as we earnestly pray that God will be towards us. Peter was concerned with this problem of forgiveness and asked Jesus if he was doing the right thing if he continued to forgive his brother after as many as seven times for doing the same thing. Jesus said that not just seven times was enough but seventy times seven, in other words you should never say 'Ah well, I have forgiven you 490 times and that's it, if you do it again you've had it!' Forgive. . . forgive . . . , forgive . . . , help, advise, encourage but still forgive.

Let us pray:

O Holy and ever-blessed Lord, teach us, we beseech thee, to love one another, to exercise forbearance and forgiveness towards our enemies; to recompense no man evil for evil, but to be merciful even as thou, our Father in heaven, art merciful: that so we may continually follow after thee in all our doings and be more and more conformed to thine image and likeness. Amen.

A Book of Prayers for Schools

4. Foundations

There are very few of us who have not stopped for at least a few minutes at some time or other to watch men at work on a building site. What fascinates us most often is the construction of the parts of the building we cannot see when it is completed . . . , the foundations. The analogy of a building and its foundations can be applied to nearly every department of life. Much that is essential to the finished product is hardly given a mention after completion. The concert pianist never practises his scales publicly. If Sir Laurence Olivier could not read, acting would be more difficult for him. Before you can understand a French newspaper you must know how to conjugate the verb *être*. The idea of foundations applies to life itself; if you are to make a success of it you must have a solid basis on which to build.

HYMN: *Glorious things of thee are spoken.*

When talking to his followers Jesus always illustrated his points with examples from the daily experience of first-century Palestine. For us in the twentieth century some things which were 'everyday' in the first century need a great deal of explanation before we can see what Jesus was getting at, but on other occasions the illustration is as familiar now as it was two thousand years ago. The parable I am going to read is one of the easy-to-understand type. Jesus said:

'Everyone who comes to me and hears what I say, and acts upon it—I will show you what he is like. He is like a man who, in building his house, dug deep and laid the foundations on rock. When the flood came, the river burst upon that house, but could not shift it, because it had been soundly built. But he who hears and does not act is like a man who built his house on the soil without foundations. As soon as the river burst upon it, the house collapsed, and fell with a great crash.'

Luke 6.47–9

We do not have to be master builders to know how true are the illustrations Jesus used. Any juvenile, or adult, builder of sand castles will testify to the destructive power of even a very small wave. Jesus meant this illustration to apply to life in general. If you are going to survive in any trouble which may afflict you it is essential to have one or two things you are very, very sure about so that even when everything else has gone wrong and let you down you can point to these few things and say 'I am sure of this . . . I know that is true . . . I firmly believe so and so?' If you have no such basis, or your basis is a false one, then trouble, when and if it comes will be overwhelming. What do I consider a false basis? Money, Power, Social Position, Friends . . . , the latter form a firmer basis than the other three but who has never been let down by so-called friends at one time or another.

The Rock of Ages, as we sing in the hymn, Jesus Christ, is the only really firm foundation upon which to base one's whole life.

Let us pray:

O God, who art the same today, yesterday and for ever give us grace and courage that we may build our lives on the sure foundations of the teaching and example of thy son, Jesus Christ, our Lord. Amen.

5. Last first, first last

It is often a source of great annoyance to us that we can be in only one place at any given moment in time. People often wish they could 'turn the clock back' a few years or forward a few years. We are human and we cannot do these things. God is subject to neither time nor space. When it comes to thinking about God this makes for difficulties but our hymn makes the eternal nature of God a subject for praise.

HYMN: *Immortal, invisible, God only wise.*

As we have seen before the point of parables can be completely missed, especially in our material age. The one we are going to examine this morning has been regarded as *the* passage in the Bible which refutes trade unionism!

'The kingdom of Heaven is like this. There was once a landowner who went out early one morning to hire labourers for his vineyard; and after agreeing to pay them the usual day's wage he sent them off to work. Going out three hours later he saw some more men standing idle in the market-place. "Go and join the others in the vineyard," he said, "and I will pay you a fair wage"; so off they went. At noon he went out again, and at three in the afternoon, and made the same arrangement as before. An hour before sunset he went out and found another group standing there; so he said to them, "Why are you standing about like this all day with nothing to do?" "Because no one has hired us", they replied; so he told them, "Go and join the others in the vineyard." When evening fell, the owner of the vineyard said to his steward, "Call the labourers and give them their pay, beginning with those who came last and ending with the first." Those who had started work an hour before sunset came forward, and were paid the day's wage. When it was the turn of, the men who had come first, they expected something extra but were paid the same amount as the others. As they took it, they grumbled at their employer: "These late-comers have done only one hour's work, yet you have put them on a level with is, who have sweated the whole day long in the blazing sun!" The owner turned to one of them and said, "My friend, I am not being unfair to you. You agreed on the usual wage for the day, did you not? Take your pay and go home. I chose to pay the last man the same as you. Surely I am free to do what I like with my own money. Why be jealous because I am kind?" Thus will the last be first, and the first last.'

Matthew 20.1–16

'This proves', say people who use this argument 'that an employer can do what he likes and the workers must make their own individual agreements and stick to them no matter what.' Rubbish! The question of labour relations has nothing whatever to do with this parable. Here we come back to what I said at first this morning. God and his Kingdom are not bound by time, they are eternal. Imagine an elderly man who has lived a good Christian life for seventy years, and a young man of twenty only recently converted to Christianity; they both die. Our earthly idea of fairness and justice demands that the old man be rewarded more than the young fellow. Jesus tells us this is not so. One is either in the Kingdom of Heaven or out of it, there are no such things as good places, and poor places, six bobs and one-and-nines! Everything and everybody is equal. 'The first shall be last and the last first'; all ideas based on a concept of time have to be forgotten. Time, days, hours, minutes, cannot apply to eternity.

Let us pray:

This prayer was written by the poet-priest John Donne who tries to capture in words some idea of the eternal nature of heaven:

Bring us, O Lord God, at our last awakening into the house and gate of heaven, to enter into that gate and dwell in that house, where there shall be no darkness nor dazzling, but one equal light; no noise nor silence, but one equal music; no fears nor hopes, but one equal possession; no ends nor beginnings, but one equal eternity; in the habitations of thy majesty and thy glory, world without end. Amen.

Memorials, from a Sermon of JOHN DONNE

6. Lost and Found

One of the things that annoyed the Pharisees and other Jewish religious leaders was the way Jesus associated himself with those who were regarded as outcasts from respectable Jewish society. For the strict Jew a sinner was a person who did not even attempt to live his life according to the letter of every single minute detail of the Laws of Moses.

By way of answer to these criticisms Jesus told the following famous parable:

'If one of you has a hundred sheep and loses one of them, does he not leave the ninety-nine in the open pasture and go after the missing one until he has found it? How delighted he is then! He lifts it on to his shoulders, and home he goes to call his friends and neighbours together. "Rejoice with me!" he cries. "I have found my lost sheep." In the same way, I tell you, there will be greater joy in heaven over one sinner who repents than over ninety-nine righteous people who do not need to repent'. *Luke 15.3–7*

We are inclined to think of sheep as rather stupid animals and shepherds not really much more intelligent. So the idea of calling Jesus the 'Good Shepherd' may appear rather insulting. But this is a case where a knowledge of animal husbandry as practised in Palestine in the time of Christ makes it possible for us to understand why he chose to regard himself as a shepherd. Sheep grazed on the open hillside where a little scrubby grass could be found. As good pasture was scarce the sheep were very dependent upon their shepherd who spent every hour of every day with them. Where the shepherd led the sheep followed. In England sheep are driven but Jesus spoke of a shepherd leading; the sheep could recognise their dependence and follow or else they could go off by themselves. Thus Jesus saw himself as the shepherd of men; leading the way, not compelling or driving men but inviting all to follow if they wish.

This parable tells of a sheep who did not follow the shepherd. Now anybody who has lost one of a set will know that one does not just say 'Ah well, I've still got the rest . . . , one does not matter' but one looks for it. The shepherd felt that way about his flock. The lost sheep represented only one per cent of his property but it was important to him. The ninety nine were all well and safe. The Pharisees were to a certain extent righteous but Jesus explains that God is not satisfied to say that he is content with ninety-nine fairly good people; he is concerned about the bad one, and is very happy when that one reforms.

It is the function of the Church to make evil men good; it is not a club for the exclusive use of the good men, it is a repair shop for the not so good. Perhaps some people within the Church are like the Pharisees and object to the contacts some of their members have with social outcasts. These people are wrong; just as wrong as the people who regard the Church as a club for the 'holy'.

HYMN: *The King of Love my shepherd is.*

Let us pray:

O Lord Jesus Christ who once called yourself the Good Shepherd, make us willing to follow you, the way, the truth and the life, so that we may form part of the great flock for whom you laid down your life. We ask this for your name's sake. Amen.

7. Prayer

'I don't know what to do ..., I don't know which way to turn ...,
I've asked the advice of all my friends ..., I've talked it over
with Dad..., I've even prayed.' 'I've even prayed'! This seems to
be a common attitude to prayer. When all else has failed, as a last
resort, pray.

HYMN: *Father hear the prayer we offer.*

Besides teaching his disciples what we call the Lord's Prayer
Jesus told a number of parables about prayer. Let us look at two of
these parables in a little detail. In the first one Luke tells us what
point Jesus was making:

> He spoke to them in a parable to show that they should keep
> on praying and never lose heart: 'There was once a judge
> who cared nothing for God or man, and in the same town
> there was a widow who constantly came before him demand-
> ing justice against her opponent. For a long time he refused;
> but in the end he said to himself, "True, I care nothing for
> God or man; but this widow is so great a nuisance that I will
> see her righted before she wears me out with her persistence."'
>
> *Luke 18.1–5*

Judges were always open to bribes and the one in this story was
much more interested in his fee than in seeing justice done. A
widow in Palestine would be very poor indeed (remember the
parable about the widow's farthing) and so would not be able to
pay much by way of fee. The judge seeing there was nothing in
the case for him ignored the widow to get on with more lucrative
cases. But, and this is the point of the parable, she kept on asking;
she was persistent and so at last her case was heard.

93

We can apply the teaching of this parable to our own day by saying that prayer must be a continual activity if it is to be effective. If somebody with the attitude to prayer given before the hymn had his request granted we would be led to think of God as a great barrel of goodness. If anybody turns the tap, that is prays, he can draw off some goodness; then when he has had enough he can turn off the tap again. Prayer has been called conversation with God. Through conversation one gets to know people and as knowledge increases so the conversations become more interesting and worthwhile. It is not possible to walk up to a complete stranger and have a good conversation with him; personal relationships take time to build up and man's relationship to God is a personal relationship.

'Keep on praying and never lose heart.'

'Of course we always go to church on Sunday morning; it wouldn't seem right if we didn't; mind you there's a rather odd couple who come sometimes, not regularly like us, they look rather uncomfortable in church. I'm not surprised really 'cos I'm sure he's the fellow who empties our dustbins and I've heard she works in a public house; not that I'd ever go in such a place myself. It'll be a pity if we have too many of that sort of people in our church. They're not really what I'd call "our class" at all.'

> 'Two men went up to the temple to pray, one a Pharisee and the other a tax-gatherer. The Pharisee stood up and prayed thus: "I thank thee, O God, that I am not like the rest of men, greedy, dishonest, adulterous; or, for that matter, like this tax-gatherer. I fast twice a week; I pay tithes on all that I get." But the other kept his distance and would not even raise his eyes to heaven, but beat upon his breast, saying, "O God, have mercy on me, sinner that I am." *Luke 18.10–14*

Saint Luke said of this parable 'It was aimed at those who were sure of their own goodness and looked down on everyone else.'

We may not have 'Pharisees and despised tax-gatherers' today but the attitude of some to others is no different. Humility is essential before we even think of praying. Before God everybody is a sinner; there is not a single person, saint or criminal, who has ever spent a whole day so perfectly that he could do absolutely no better. Two essentials in prayer are humility and persistence.

Let us pray:

O Lord Jesus Christ who by your example and in your parables has taught us that the greatest of all is the servant of all and that the humble shall be exalted, help us always to be humble enough to realise our dependence upon God so that we may persist in our prayers of praise and thanksgiving, of confession for our shortcomings and of requests for others and for ourselves; we ask this in your name Jesus Our Lord and Our God. Amen.

8. The Speck and the Plank

So often we are told to read our Bibles; less often we try and then soon give it up. Why? The usual answer is 'I can't understand what it's all about.'

There are two main difficulties:

First, the audience originally addressed were Hebrew peasants of about two thousand years ago; and second, the ideas are always expressed in very general terms apparently remote from our own situation.

There is nothing much we can do about the first difficulty but the answer to the second is to apply the idea expressed to our lives. To gain anything of real value from Bible-reading we must do three things. Read. Analyse. Apply.

HYMN: *Lord thy word abideth, and our footsteps guideth.*

The last verse of the hymn tells us that through discerning, that is, taking notice of, the word of God, primarily the Bible, we may come to love God and hear what advice he has to give us.

I am now going to read a few verses from St. Luke's Gospel; and say what I think each group of verses means; and suggest ways this can be applied to our lives; that is I am going to read, analyse, and apply.

'Why do you look at the speck of sawdust in your brother's eye, with never a thought for the great plank in your own? How can you say to your brother, "My dear brother, let me take the speck out of your eye", when you are blind to the plank in your own? You hypocrite! First take the plank out of

your own eye, and then you will see clearly to take the speck
out of your brothers'.   *Luke 6.41–2*

Here we have one person criticising another when he has no
right, and in a very superior manner. His trouble is that he thinks
that he is perfect and so from the height of his perfection he lowers
himself to help the other man. But he is not perfect, he has faults
which stand out so much that they could not be more obvious if he
actually had a great plank is his eye. The lesson to be learned from
this parable is that we should not say anything about other people
until we have had a good look at ourselves. The examination of
our own behaviour often reveals faults similar to those we were
about to condemn in another. We should condemn the fault but
in ourselves. Other people will notice soon enough if we correct
it.

'There is no such thing as a good tree producing worthless
fruit, nor yet a worthless tree producing good fruit. For each
tree is known by its own fruit: you do not gather figs from
thistles, and you do not pick grapes from brambles. A good
man produces good from the store of good within himself;
and an evil man from evil within produces evil. For the words
that the mouth utters come from the overflowing of the
heart.'   *Luke 6.43–4*

It has been said that if one goes on doing something for long
enough one will convince oneself that it is all right, even though at
first it seemed to be wrong. Fortunately we are not like the trees in
this parable because we can choose whether to do good or evil. But
we are to be judged by what we actually do. So if we always do
evil things then we must be evil. Before we do any action, speak
any sentence, we must ask ourselves whether it is a good or a bad
thing to say or to do. We can then choose. Sometimes we will find
it easier to do good than to do evil. Sometimes it will be hard. When
we do not know whether a thing is good or evil we can ask somebody whose judgement we respect. But all the time, though our
actions show we are good or evil people, we can always choose the

standards upon which we base our behaviour; basic standards of good will produce good; basic standards of evil will produce evil.

Let us pray:

Almighty and most merciful God, who hast given the Bible to be the revelation of thy great love to man and of thy power and will to save him: grant that by it we may be lifted to hope, made strong for service, and, above all, filled with the true knowledge of thee and of thy Son Jesus Christ. Amen.

GEORGE ADAM SMITH *A Book of Prayers for Schools*

9. Talents

We use the word talent today to refer to a special aptitude or gift some people have for doing various things; acting, singing, playing football and so forth. We are also told that we each have some talent; there are one or two things at which we find we are more successful than any other things we turn our hand to. In the time of Christ the word 'talent' referred to a large sum of money, but it is from one of his parables that we derive the modern meaning of the word.

HYMN: *Teach me, my God and King.*

This is the parable Jesus told about talents:
'The Kingdom of Heaven is like a man going abroad, who called his servants and put his capital in their hands; to one he gave five bags of gold, to another two, to another one, each according to his capacity. Then he left the country. The man who had the five bags went at once and employed them in business, and made a profit of five bags, and the man who had the two bags made two. But the man who had been given one bag of gold went off and dug a hole in the ground, and hid his master's money. A long time afterwards their master returned, and proceeded to settle accounts with them. The man who had been given the five bags of gold came and produced the five he had made: "Master," he said, "you left five bags with me; look, I have made five more." "Well done, my good and trusty servant!" said the master "You have proved trustworthy in a small way; I will now put you in charge of something big. Come and share your master's delight." The man with the

two bags then came and said, "Master, you left two bags with me; look, I have made two more." 'Well done, my good and trusty servant!" said the master. "You have proved trustworthy in a small way; I will now put you in charge of something big. Come and share your master's delight." Then the man who had been given one bag came and said, "Master, I knew you to be a hard man: you reap where you have not sown, you gather where you have not scattered; so I was afraid, and I went and hid your gold in the ground. Here it is —you have what belongs to you." "You lazy rascal!" said the master. "You knew that I reap where I have not sown, and I gather where I have not scattered? Then you ought to have put my money on deposit, and on my return I should have got it back with interest. Take the bag of gold from him, and give it to the one with the ten bags. For the man who has will always be given more, till he has enough and to spare; and the man who has not will forfeit even what he has." '

Matthew 25.14–29

Some people regard this parable as a complete justification capitalism, with its stocks and shares, high finance and big business, but this is to consider only the story and to ignore the meaning behind the story. If you remember the point of a parable is to make difficult points clear for simple people it is not difficult to see that it is perfectly possible for a man to use money to make more money.

When we leave the field of finance and think of 'talent' in the modern sense it is harder to check up on how much use has been made of the particular gifts of an individual; that is, hard for us to do for *others*. We each know whether *we* are making the fullest use of our own talents, and we all have them to a greater or lesser degree; and besides this God knows what use we have made of his gifts. Notice we now speak of gifts; gifts must be given, *by* somebody *to* somebody. Our difficulty is to discover what talents we have and then it is our duty both to God and to our fellow human beings to do all we can to train and to use our talents to the best of our ability. Bobby Charlton is a talented footballer but he has to train hard to achieve his best, Yehudi Menuhin is a talented violinist and he has to practise. But it is not just practice; some of your teachers could train for as many hours as Charlton and still not be picked to play for the Staff against the School; or we could practise for as many hours as Menuhin and still be asked *not* to play the violin.

The message of this parable is that we should make the fullest possible use of *our* talents even though they may not be very great or numerous. Our best is the most we can do, and we must see that we do it at all times.

Let us pray:

O Everlasting God, who from all eternity dost behold and order all things, and hast called us to serve thee in this our generation, doing the work of God after the manner of men: Enable us so to use the talents entrusted to us, to thy glory and the service of others, that at the last we may hear that most joyful voice, Well done, thou good and faithful servant, enter thou into the joy of thy Lord; through the same our Saviour Jesus Christ. Amen.

JEREMY TAYLOR (adapted)

10. Total Selfishness

HYMN: *Awake my soul and with the sun.*

Parables are 'word pictures' and in the one I am going to read this morning it is more important than usual to remember this. The story concerns a man who in his lifetime was completely selfish. In painting his word picture Jesus uses ideas popular in Palestine in his day, about heaven and hell. It is quite wrong to regard these illustrations as authentic eye-witness accounts to the pleasures of heaven or the torments of hell. Jesus is making the story as vivid as possible for his original hearers.

"There was once a rich man, who dressed in purple and the finest linen, and feasted in great magnificence every day. At his gate, covered with sores, lay a poor man named Lazarus, who would have been glad to satisfy his hunger with the scraps from the rich man's table. Even the dogs used to come and lick his sores. One day the poor man died and was carried away by the angels to be with Abraham. The rich man also died and was buried, and in Hades, where he was in torment, he looked up; and there, far away, was Abraham with Lazarus close beside him. "Abraham, my father," he called out, "take pity on me! Send Lazarus to dip the tip of his finger in water, to cool my tongue, for I am in agony in this fire." But Abraham said, "Remember, my child, that all the good things fell to you while you were alive, and all the bad to Lazarus; now he has his consolation here and it is you who are in agony. But that is not all: there is a great chasm fixed between us; no one from our side who wants to reach you can cross it, and none may pass from your side to us." "Then, father," he replied, "will you send him to my father's house, where I have five brothers, to warn them, so that they too may not come to this place of torment?" But Abraham said, "They have Moses and the prophets; let them listen to them." "No, father Abraham," he replied, "but if someone from the dead visits them, they will repent." Abraham answered, "If they do not listen to Moses and the prophets they will pay no heed even if someone should rise from the dead." '   *Luke 16.19–31*

Beggars were often to be found near the gates of large houses. The point here is that the rich man must have seen Lazarus day after day but never did he do anything to help him. The rich man was too busy enjoying himself. Eventually both men die; Lazarus is now the better off of the two but still the rich man's consuming interest is himself. 'Send Lazarus to dip the tip of his finger in water to cool my tongue.' Then at last the rich man thinks of somebody else besides himself . . . , his brothers. Only when his own position is utterly hopeless and there is absolutely nothing anybody can do to help him does this man think of others. The reply Abraham gives in Jesus' story seems rather harsh, but if the rich man's brothers were as much like him as we are led to believe they are likely to ignore somebody risen from the dead. After all both the rich man and his brothers had plenty of opportunity, plenty of encouragement to perform selfless acts but had done nothing except think of themselves.

The message Jesus was illustrating is quite straightforward; nobody lives for ever so make sure to do what good you can while the chance remains; tomorrow may be too late. It is not really pessimistic to repeat that tomorrow may be too late for any one of us; never be afraid of doing too much good for others. The longer you live the more opportunities you will have . . . , so beware of selfishness.

Let us pray:

O Christ, most pure and merciful and just, who came into our darkness to be our Saviour: Make us at all times and in

103

all things to love and do only that which will appear merciful, just and pure in the bright light of thy coming again to be our judge; who livest and reignest in the glory of the Eternal Trinity, world without end. Amen.

E. MILNER-WHITE: *Daily Prayer*

SAINTS

Starting in September the order of these fifteen Assemblies is that of Saints' Days in the Calendar except for John the Baptist who was dealt with in early December and the two on Saint Peter which came before and after Easter.

1. Saint Matthew

HYMN: *He sat to watch o'er customs paid.*

When somebody does something spectacular as a writer or scientist or some such the newspapers always make a great fuss of his lowly origins. It seems to be the thing to make out that one has triumphed over great difficulties to reach one's present position. One rarely hears people talking of Mr Wilson and saying he was a lecturer at Oxford for several years. No! What gets the publicity is his 'working-class background'. Often people do deserve much credit for achieving success despite their backgrounds; though they may be no better than several men who had the advantages of a well-to-do home.

Saint Matthew belonged to a group of outcasts. He was a tax-collector. Matthew's job was to collect taxes for the hated Roman soldiers, who despised him for doing it. The main trouble was that tax-collectors could charge what they liked, almost, because they bought the right to collect in a village for several hundred pounds then they collected that much back from the villagers and anything they could make on the side.

Jesus called Mathew, or Levi as he was then named, to leave his money bags and to follow him. Think what conflict must have taken place in Matthew's mind. He would be afraid that the crowd would laugh, and would the other disciples accept him as a friend? What if Jesus was not serious, would he look a fool? Could he leave all the money he had accumulated? But this man Jesus did ask him so perhaps it would be all right. Self-questioning of this sort before making a decision happens to us too time after time. Equally frequently we are afraid to take the plunge and commit ourselves whole-heartedly. Afraid to say yes; afraid to say no. At least with an oral question the questioner can ask again to press for an answer but much of life consists in each person having to act positively in situations. If I say 'Would you like to be successful?' and you reply 'I don't mind.' I can tell you that you won't be! If your vicar or minister says 'Would you like to go to heaven?' and all you can say is 'If you like.' You just won't get there. The vicar may like you to go but you must act for yourself in this case. When it comes to living a good life you can fail in two ways: firstly, by doing things you ought not to do, and secondly by not doing things that you ought to have done.

Levi, the tax-collector, was a cheat and a fraud and deservedly hated; but he became Saint Matthew, Apostle and Evangelist, servant of God. His action when Christ called him was no weak 'I-don't-mind', but he left everything there and then and followed Christ, doing what he taught at all times, looking about for opportunities to do good lest he should leave undone something he ought to have done.

Matthew overcame his background as many other men have done in all walks of life but it requires immediate and positive action and a determination to leave nothing undone which can ever romotely possible be done. Be like Matthew, act positively.

Let us pray:

O Thou who art the life of all that lives, the strength of the weak, and the hope of those that be cast down, inform our minds with thy truth, we beseech thee, and our hearts with righteousness; strengthen our wills to choose the good and to refuse the evil; help us to bear each other's burdens and to forgive one another's faults; grant this through Jesus Christ our Lord. Amen.

WILLIAM KNIGHT: *A Book of Prayers for Schools*

2. Saint Francis of Assisi

HYMN; *My God, accept my heart this day.*

Let us pray the prayer of Saint Francis of Assisi:

> Lord, make us instruments of thy peace.
> Where there is hatred, let us sow love;
> where there is injury, pardon;
> where there is discord, union;
> where there is doubt, faith;
> where there is despair, hope;
> where there is darkness, light;
> where there is sadness, joy;
> for thy mercy and for thy truth's sake.
> Amen.

The author of the prayer we have just used was the gay son of a very wealthy Italian cloth merchant. For years he enjoyed his life of ease then one day he swopped places with a beggar to see what it was like to be really poor. The more he found out about disease and poverty the more sympathetic he became. When he spent money to assist the repair of a tumble-down church his father disowned him. From that day he was called Francis of Assisi. Other men and women joined Francis and they were known as the 'Friars Minor.' that is Lesser Brothers, and travelled all over Europe helping people in need. Saint Francis was not a priest but worked among ordinary people living a Christian life which gave them help when they were in need and provided them with a practical example when they had time to think about Christianity.

By the year 1300 there were over fifty friaries in England; and there are still Friars Minor all over the world who put into practice the words of the hymn we sang. They asked God to accept their hearts.

Many of us will have very mixed feelings about the value of the Religious, that is monks and nuns, in the world today, but one of the weakest arguments against their existence is to say 'What if we all shut ourselves away in a monastery and didn't marry? What would happen to the world then?' But we are not all expected to take the three vows of poverty, chastity and obedience. We may admire various pop-singers but we do not expect everybody to be pop-singers; we may think teaching the finest profession but we do not want all the world employed in teaching.

It takes all sorts to make a world. Some sorts we could do without, but the world needs men and women who will hear Christ speaking 'and give every thought, and word, and work' to God. People who will promise to serve Christ and have him for their master and their guide.

Saint Francis taught by example, as does the Franciscan order he founded, by living and working with people. The spirit of the rule of Saint Francis is open to all of us, to try and live by, and for us to be instruments of God's peace, replacing hatred by love, discord by union, sadness by joy all the time everywhere we go.

May the Lord grant us his blessing and fill our hearts with the spirit of truth and peace, now and for evermore. Amen.

3. Saint Luke, the Doctor

Most of us are normally quite healthy; even those who score a number of absences during the term are not always really ill. It is only when we are ill or have broken a limb that we are aware of what it really means to be healthy. It is at these times too that we are aware of the work of the medical profession; doctors, nurses, chemists and scientists who carry out research into new types of drugs, and many others. It does us good now and again to reflect on the subject of health. 18 October is the feast day of the patron of all the medical profession, Saint Luke.

HYMN: *Thine arm, O Lord, in days of old.*

Luke is traditionally refered to as a doctor, and in his Gospel we get more detail of the illnesses from which people were suffering before Jesus healed them than we do from the other Gospels. Saint Paul also refers to his friend Luke as 'the dear doctor'.

Throughout the ages medicine and religion have been closely connected. Witch-doctors ancient and modern do know a little about medicine and often do cure people from certain diseases. In the mind of primitive people the knowledge of the witch-doctor gives him great power. Not unnaturally witch-doctors revel in this admiration and build up masses of rituals around their activities. Usually the more elaborate the ritual the less the doctor actually knows and the more he is trusting to luck or the more he prays to his gods.

Jesus Christ also brought together religion and medicine. The only difficulty we have in accepting the miracles of healing is the time factor—all the diseases Jesus is reported to have cured, which can be identified, can be cured by modern medicine; but over a greater period of time.

Jesus was also able to see that some diseases which looked as though they were physical were in fact mental. In the story of the sick of the palsy who was let down through the roof to Jesus, he said, 'Son thy sins be forgiven thee,' because Jesus knew that it was worry about his sins which was the cause of his paralysis.

Ill-health can be divided into three fairly distinct sections:

First, there is physical ill-health; for example mumps or measels, which are caused by some germ or other.

Second there is mental ill-health; for example amnesia, the sudden loss of memory as the result of a shock. Mental ill-health is something about which we know comparatively little and find difficult to understand; and because of this we still tend to make jokes about 'nut-houses' and 'looney-bins'. The mentally ill need our care and sympathy as much as the physically ill.

Third, there is spiritual ill-health. So little do we know about this that there are many who would not even recognise this as a separate category. War, greed, violence, discontent, dishonesty are all symptoms of spiritual ill-health. We do not need to look far to see the results of this form of ill-health. Consider the crime rate in this country, or again, many strikes are caused by the greed of some men. This brings us back to the connection between religion and medicine. 'Dr Luke' helped treat the physical ailments of his contemporaries but he has prescribed the teachings of Jesus Christ as written in his Gospel to be taken and applied for the spiritual diseases of all mankind, for all time.

Let us pray:

> Almighty God, whose blessed Son Jesus Christ went about doing good, and healing all manner of sickness and all manner of disease among the people: continue, we beseech thee, this his gracious work among us, especially in the hospitals and infirmaries of our land; cheer, heal, and sanctify the sick; grant to the physicians, surgeons, and nurses, wisdom and skill, sympathy and patience; and send down thy blessing on all who labour to prevent suffering and to forward thy purposes of love; through Jesus Christ our Lord. Amen.

1928 Prayer-Book

4. King Alfred the Great

'Huh, what's all this got to do with R.I.?' How often is this sort of thought in the minds, if not on muttered lips,in the R.I. lesson! Every single thing is 'to do with R.I.'. This is the crux of the whole subject of religion, unless it has real meaning and application to life it is a useless exercise. So it is very much a part of R.I. for a class to discuss contemporary problems and try to find out how a Christian ought to react in a given situation. A Christian is not to be judged by his ability to recite the names of the Kings of Israel and Judah from 1000BC to AD 70, but he is to be judged by the quality of life he lives.

Our hymn advises us to live life to the full and to strive continually for what is right.

HYMN: *Fight the good fight.*

In the year AD 481 when England was struggling against the Danish invasion, King Alfred came to the throne of Wessex. The Danes were not his only problems. Religion and education had declined in the years before Alfred. 'It has often come into my remembrance' he wrote 'what wise men there formerly were among the English race . . . . and how foreigners came to this land for wisdom and instruction.'

Alfred had two ambitions: to restore peace and expel the Danes, and to make England once again famous for religion and learning. He established monasteries and helped to translate books from Latin into English. He encouraged all his nobles to learn to read and write; they used to think reading and writing suitable for women and weaklings only!

Alfred revised the legal system and eventually drove out the Danes. Nobody would deny him the title 'Great'.

Law-giver, judge, statesman, author, M.P.; the men who do these jobs can be Christians too, as Alfred the Great was. Tom Driburg and Norman St John Stevas are both M.P.s belonging to different parties but they have this in common; they are practising Christians and are trying to see that this country is governed in accordance with the teaching of Christ. The work of the Church is not to provide people with an hour's entertainment on a Sunday but to make this world here and now a much better place. King Alfred did this; many Christian M.P.s are doing this and you and I can do this by putting the teaching of Jesus Christ into practice to the best of our ability all day and every day.

Let us pray:

> We remember before thee, O God, the leaders of our nation, those who govern in the affairs of Church and State, those who control industry and commerce, those who educate men's minds through literature and those who through positions of influence or wealth control the destinies of others. Grant that they may at all times seek the guidance of thy Holy Spirit; direct and control their councils that, fearless and unfaltering, they may stand for all that is good and true and further thy kingdom in the realms of this world. Amen.

W. L. ANDERSON: A Book of Prayers for Schools

5. Saint John the Baptist

'Repent ye for the Kingdom of Heaven is at hand.' This is what John the Baptist shouted when he preached near the River Jordan in about AD 27 Saint John the Baptist is the only Christian saint to be remembered on the anniversary of his birth rather than of his death.

HYMN: *On Jordan's bank the Baptist's cry.*

We all use symbols of various kinds every day. In Maths an answer may begin 'Let X be the number of people who. . . '. X is a symbol. Motorists make use, we hope of all sorts of symbols. In all cases we have got to know what they stand for if they are to be of any value. And it is easy enough to make up ideas for which a given symbol might stand, for example, 'Danger camels crossing' might be taken for 'Humped back bridge', or 'Did you close the front gate?' for 'Level crossing'.

Baptism is also a symbol which has a special meaning. This was not apparent to the two-year-old boy who on being taken to the font squeaked appealingly 'No bathies, no bathies.'

So what was John the Baptist playing at ducking people in the rather mucky Jordan River? What does baptism stand for today, whether it is the gentle sprinkling or the one. . . two. . . three. . . under type?

John was using Baptism as a symbol for people who wished to turn over a new leaf in preparation for the coming Messiah. An outward act to symbolise a spiritual change in their lives. I am not going to discuss infant and adult baptism but I will say that we must be careful to make sure that we do not just *do* things but

E

know, and find out if we do not know, what various actions symbolise.

Road accidents are often the result of people not knowing the meaning of symbols. Ignorance of other symbols can have all sorts of far-reaching and unexpected results. Jesus was betrayed by Judas who kissed him; an example of the misuse of a widely accepted symbol of friendship. Wearing crosses and crucifixes, and making the sign of the cross, are symbols of allegiance to Jesus Christ. Wearing black is a symbol of mourning for the dead. John the Baptist believed strongly in telling the truth; it was because of Herod Antipas' immorality for which John publicly rebuked him that John was imprisoned.

The messages of John for us today seems to me to be:

First, check that we know the meaning of any symbols we use, or come across or do, or say.

Second, to make sure we are always sincere in our use of these symbols.

Let us pray:

O Lord Our God, save us from unreality, from praising what is good while practising what is bad; from thinking high thoughts while living a poor life. Keep us from ignoble fear and send us on our way with hope; through Jesus Christ our Lord. Amen.

A Book of Prayers for Schools

6. Saint Nicolas

Only a few shopping days to Christmas; but all the same it seems rather early to be celebrating and singing Christmas carols and hymns. However if you lived in Holland, 6 December not the 25th would be the day you would wake up to find a stocking, or rather clog, full of presents from Santa Claus. Santa Claus is an American version of the Dutch dialect form of Saint Nicolas, Sinte Klaus.

HYMN: *O, Little town of Bethlehem.*

Who was Saint Nicolas? History can tell us very little but legend has much to say. Certainly he was a very popular saint in the seventh to the ninth centuries because there are many churches dating from that time dedicated to him. The only definite fact is that in the early years of the fourth century the town of Myra in Asia Minor, modern Turkey, was served by a Bishop called Nicolas.

Nicolas is the patron saint of sailors, children, pawnbrokers, among others. Legend tells of the times he saved sailors who ran aground on the coast near his town. A more detailed legend goes like this: There was a very poor family in Myra who had three daughters. The mother died and the father became ill. Things went from bad to worse and it looked as though thy would all be thrown into the debtors' prison. The good Bishop got to hear of this and so went secretly one night to the poor man's house and threw in through the window three bags of gold. Another legend which seems to be connected with three bags of gold is that three small boys were murdered by suffocation by having bags tied over their heads. After appeal to Saint Nicolas the boys' bodies were found in a large barrel and brought to life by him.

117

The connection with pawnbrokers seems to come from the three bags of gold which could be arranged in art to look like the three balls of the pawnbrokers' sign.

The points which seem to survive the legends are first that Nicolas was a generous man, second that he was fond of children and third that he tried to do his good deeds secretly.

At this time of the year we give presents but unlike Nicolas we have a tendency to give only to people we know will give to us. But this is not in the spirit of Saint Nicolas, or of Christ. Both disciple and master advocate giving to those who really need without thought of return.

When you see a red-nosed Santa grinning at you from shop window advertisements remember Saint Nicolas, the Bishop, and when you see the word Christmas do not forget the Christ part of it. This will help you to find the true spirit of the festival.

Let us pray:

Almighty God, bestow upon us, we beseech thee, such love and charity as were his, to whom it was more blessed to give than to receive, and who came not to be ministered unto, but to minister. May the same mind be in us as was also in Jesus Christ, while we keep the festival of his divine humility, consecrating ourselves to the service of all who are in need; for the sake of Jesus Christ our Lord. Amen.

A Chain of Prayer Across the Ages

7. Innocents' Day

Christmas means to most of us presents and parties, eating and drinking; a time of rejoicing on the anniversary of the birth of Jesus Christ. But as early as the time of Jesus' second birthday there was an occasion of great sadness and suffering in addition to the rejoicing.

Saint Matthew records it like this:

'Herod . . . fell into a passion and gave orders for the massacre of all children in Bethlehem and its neighbourhood of the age of two years or less.'

This horrible event is remembered on 28 December and it is about this less happy aspect of Christmas we are going to think this morning.

HYMN: *Unto us a boy is born.*

Tradition gives the number of boys killed as twenty-six. The name given to them, 'Innocents', reminds us of the obvious fact that they had done nothing wrong themselves; none of them was plotting against King Herod.

In a poem Norman Nicholson describes the first Innocents' Day from the point of view of Herod:

'And Herod said—Supposing you had been in my shoes, what would you have done different?—I was not thinking of myself. This Child—whichever number might have come from the hat—could

Scarcely have begun to make trouble for twenty or
Thirty years at least, and by that time
Ten to one I'd be dead and gone.'

Herod the Great was allowed by the Romans who had conquered Palestine to continue as King of Judea; but he had to toe the line; he was more or less a puppet-king. The Romans thought Herod was more likely to keep peace in that corner of their Empire than they could by themselves. Herod realized that any revolution in Palestine would be put down severely by the Romans and the Jews most likely exterminated. Nicholson's poem concludes:

> 'If that child had lived,
> Not a stone would have stayed on a stone, nor a brother with
>   brother,
> Nor would all the Babylons of all the world
> Have had water enough to swill away the tears.
> *That*
> I have put a stop to, at the price
> Of a two-year crop of children, making
> What future observers will undoubtedly judge a
> Good bargain with history.'

Of course the boy he hoped to kill escaped and grew to manhood to preach peace, 'Love your enemies; do good to those who treat you spitefully.' It also happened that in the time of Herod's great-grandson there was a rebellion and Jerusalem was destroyed and the Jews were scattered all over the world.

The tragedy of the Massacre of the Innocents has three aspects:

First the needless waste of twenty-six innocent lives and the grief of their families.

Second the fact that what Herod aimed to prevent, a revolution fatal to the Jewish nation, happened within seventy or so years.

Third this is the most tragic of all, that Herod thought he was doing the right thing.

It is this third point that we would do well to take to heart. 'I meant to help.' 'I thought that was what you were supposed to do.' We have all made remarks like this after something has gone wrong. Practically everything we do is going to affect others and we owe it to them, to ourselves and to God who gave us brains, to think and think hard before we do anything which involves the happiness or safety of other people.

Let us pray:

O God, our Father, by whom we have been so wonderfully created, enable us to so use the minds we have been given that in all we say and do we may seek the guidance of the Holy Spirit through thought and prayer. Help us also to be humble enough to seek and heed advice from our fellow men and when necessary to change our minds without thought of selfish pride. We ask these things in the name of Jesus Christ that we may live our lives in accordance with the pattern he gave us in his perfect life on earth. Amen.

8. Saint Paul

HYMN: *Praise to the Lord, the Almighty, the King of creation.*

Let us pray:

> We remember before thee, O God, the leaders of our nation, those who govern in the affairs of Church and State, those who control industry and commerce, those who educate men's minds through literature and the press, who through positions of influence or wealth control the destinies of others. Grant that they may at all times seek the guidance of thy Holy Spirit; direct and control their councils that, fearless and unfaltering, they may stand for all that is good and true and further thy kingdom in the realms of this world. Amen.

W. L. ANDERSON

In our prayer we have just remembered before God people in authority or positions of power who have responsibilities towards their fellow-men. Obviously they must not misuse their power. But ordinary people like ourselves must not be too thick either. We must be aware of the circumstances of those in authority who want us to do things. When a man suggests a certain course of action knowing he will benefit from it, or opposes a certain course of action because he will suffer, we refer to his concern as a 'vested interest'. Imagine the chairman of a housing committee who advises the building of one thousand houses on a certain plot of land. He does not tell everybody that he owns the plot of land he is suggesting and would stand to make enormous financial gains. He has a vested interest in seeing that the houses are built on his land.

Saint Paul came up against 'vested interests' when he preached Christianity in Ephesus. Notice in the story we are about to hear how:

First the silversmiths make use of the ordinary people in Ephesus to protect their 'vested interests'.

Second the people are unaware that they are being used.

Third, the Town Clerk is astute enough to see what has so incensed the silversmiths and calms the people without actually exposing either the dishonesty of the silversmiths or the gullibility of the crowd. A true diplomat.

'Now about that time, the Christian movement gave rise to a serious disturbance. There was a man named Demetrius, a silversmith who made silver shrines of Diana and provided a great deal of employment for the craftsmen. He called a meeting of these men and the workers in allied trades, and addressed them. 'Men,' he said, 'you know that our high standard of living depends on this industry. And you see and hear how this fellow Paul with his propaganda has perverted crowds of people, not only at Ephesus but also in practically the whole of the province of Asia. He is telling them that gods made by human hands are not gods at all. There is danger for us here; it is not only that the sanctuary of the great goddess Diana will cease to command respect; and then it will not be long before she who is worshipped by all Asia and the civilized world is brought down from her divine pre-eminence.'

When they heard this they were roused to fury and shouted, 'Great is Diana of the Ephesians!' The whole city was in confusion; they seized Paul's travelling-companions, the Macedonians Gaius and Aristarchus, and made a concerted rush with them into the theatre. Paul wanted to appear before the assembly but the other Christians would not let him. Even some of the dignitaries of the province, who were friendly towards him, sent and urged him not to venture into the theatre. Meanwhile some were shouting one thing, some another; for the assembly was in confusion and most of them did not know what they had all come for. But some of the crowd explained the trouble to Alexander, whom the Jews had pushed to the front, and he, motioning for silence, attempted to make a defence before the assembly. But when they recognized that he was a Jew, a single cry arose from them all: for abut two hours they kept on shouting, 'Great is Diana of the Ephesians!'

The town clerk, however, quieted the crowd. 'Men of Ephesus,' he said, 'all the world knows that our city of Ephesus is temple warden of the great Diana and of that symbol of her which fell from heaven. Since these facts are beyond dispute, your proper course is to keep quiet and do nothing rash. These men whom you have brought here as culprits have committed no sacrilege and uttered no blasphemy against our goddness. If therefore Demetrius and his craftsmen have a case against anyone, assizes are held and there are such people as proconsuls; let the parties bring their charges and countercharges. If, on the other hand, you have some further question to raise, it will be dealt with in the statutory assembly. We certainly run the risk of being charged with riot for this day's work. There is no justification for it, and if the issue is raised we shall be unable to give any explanation of this uproar.' With that he dismissed the assembly.'

Acts 19.23–41

9. Saint Valentine

HYMN:, *O, worship the King*.

The English language is very rich and has a word which fits most shades of meaning or express most ideas; but not quite in *every* case. There is the word 'love'. This is used in dozens of different ways to express dozens of ideas.

For example:

'I love ice-cream.'
'You love your mother.'
'He loves the girl next door.'
'She loves children.'
'God is love.'
'Love your neighbour.'

If we try to picture the people concerned in any of the first four sentences we imagine them to be happy, and smiling, and looking as though they mean what they say. But when it comes to the last two the scene changes: black suits, long, grey faces totally devoid of a sense of fun loom up in our minds. Why is this? Is the love of God really unconnected with love we have for people and things of this world? Far from it! God's love is the foundation for all the other types of love. The church is often referred to as the bride of Christ and he died for the Church; that is love of the highest order. The first miracle Jesus performed was, according to Saint John's Gospel, at a wedding. There the love of two people for each other was witnessed by Jesus who shared the festivities. Saint Valentine, a Bishop of the third century, has become the patron saint of lovers.

Perhaps the reason why we run from the love of God is that we feel he has given, and still gives, so much that our weak efforts at loving others make us ashamed of ourselves. It is a common attitude today to decry what you do not understand. This is a wrong attitude, and we are wrong if we regard the love of God in austere and unlovely terms merely because we do not understand it. God's love, then, is the basis of all the love in the world; listen to some thoughts of Saint John on the subject:

God is love; he who dwells in love is dwelling in God, and God in him. This is for us the perfection of love, to have confidence on the day of judgement, and this we can have, because even in this world we are as he is. There is no room for fear in love; perfect love banishes fear. For fear brings with it the pains of judgement, and anyone who is afraid has not attained to love in its perfection. We love because he loved us first. But if a man says, 'I love God', while hating his brother, he is a liar. If he does not love the brother whom he has seen, it cannot be that he loves God whom he has not seen. And indeed this command comes to us from Christ himself: that he who loves God must also love his brother.

I John 4.16b–21

Let us ask God to bless and help us in all our efforts in loving.

Let us pray for our families and friends:

O God, we thank thee this day for our homes and the loving influence of our parents, for our brothers and sisters, our relations and our friends, and for all who by their life and example have helped us to know more of thee. Grant us to show forth our gratitude in willing service, that in the love of the brotherhood we may make perfect the love that is in thee; through Jesus Christ our Lord. Amen.

W. L. ANDERSON: *A Book of Prayers for Schools*

10. Mary, Mother of Jesus

HYMN: *Christ whose glory fills the skies.*

Most primitive religions worship a goddess. The art of such societies shows the truth of this. Christians refer to their God as 'he'. Father, Son and Holy Spirit are all thought of as male. But Jesus Christ was born as a man and so had to have a mother. Some accuse the Roman Catholics of making Mary a goddess; but do non-Catholics always do justice to this human woman who was chosen to be the mother of God? There are three main sources of information about 'Mary the mother of the Lord': first, The New Testament, second, the Apocryphal Gospels written in about the ninth century AD and third, traditional stories handed down over the years. Tradition says that Mary's parents, Anna and Joakin, were both of the tribe of David and natives of Bethlehem and Nazareth. Everybody knows the stories connected with the birth of Jesus as recorded in the Gospels of Matthew and Luke. But here are a few other isolated verses which have a lot to say about the character of this remarkable woman.

'But Mary kept all these things pondering them in her heart.'

Luke 2.19

This refers to all the wonderful things connected with Jesus' early life, the shepherds, the Kings, the doctors in the Temple—typical of a mother!

Saint John records the first miracle that Jesus performed which was to turn water into wine at a wedding in Cana. John begins the story by saying:

'There was a marriage at Cana-in-Galilee and the mother of Jesus was there.'

It is Mary who brings the news of the lack of wine to Jesus, hoping that he can do something about it.

Jesus spent three years travelling up and down Palestine teaching and preaching. Saint Mark records on one occasion that a message is brought in to Jesus:

'And his mother and his brothers came and standing outside they sent to him and called him.'

His mother is keen to see that Jesus is well. She is concerned for his welfare. She knows he is arousing the opposition of the Pharisees. Her concern is that of every mother for her child.

That Jesus held his mother in highest regard is seen by the fact that he always wished to protect her from being hurt or involved in his clash with the Jewish religious leaders. The most famous occasion was when Jesus was suffering on the cross, on the point of death, he sees his mother and his good friend and disciple, John, and says:

'Woman behold your son; (indicating John) then he said to the disciple behold your mother.'

There are many stories about the rest of Mary's life.

On 'Lady Day' we commemorate the occasion on which Mary first knew she was to be the mother of Jesus.

We are asked to follow the teaching of Jesus and his example. Let us remember him and his relations with his parents in all our dealings with our own parents.

Let us pray in the words of a hymn:

Joy to be Mother of the Lord,
And hers the truer bliss,
In every thought and deed and word
To be for ever his,
And as he loves thee, Mother dear,
We too will love thee well;
And, to his glory, year by year,
Thy joy and honour tell.
Amen.

11. Saint Peter (i) The Coward

Of the Twelve Apostles of Jesus, Simon Peter is the one about whom we have most information. He reveals himself not as a perfect man like Jesus but as a person of great potential goodness with enormous energy not always used in the right directions. We ordinary folk can learn from the mistakes of the great as well as from their good deeds. Today we are going to read about an action of Simon Peter's which made him thoroughly ashamed.

HYMN: *Be thou my guardian and my guide.*

> After singing the Passover Hymn, they went out to the Mount of Olives. Then Jesus said to them, 'Tonight you will all fall from your faith on my account; for it stands written "I will strike the shepherd down and the sheep of his flock will be scattered." But after I am raised again, I will go on before you into Galilee.' Peter replied, 'Everyone else may fall away on your account, but I never will.' Jesus said to him, 'I tell you, tonight before the cock crows you will disown me three times. Peter said, 'Even if I must die with you, I will never disown you.' And all the disciples said the same.
>
> *Matt. 26.30–5*

After waiting some time in the garden Jesus was arrested by a company of the Temple Guards led by Judas. All the disciples ran away.

> The chief priests and the whole Council tried to find some allegation against Jesus on which a death-sentence could be based; but they failed to find one, though many came forward with false evidence. Finally two men alleged that he had said 'I can pull down the temple of God, and rebuild it in three days.' At this the High Priest rose and said to him, 'Have you no answer to the charge that these witnesses bring against you?' But Jesus kept silence. The High Priest then said, 'By the

living God I charge you to tell us: Are you the Messiah, the Son of God?' Jesus replied. 'The words are yours. But I tell you this: from now on, you will see the Son of Man seated at the right hand of God and coming on the clouds of heaven.' At these words the High Priest tore his robes and exclaimed, 'Blasphemy! Need we call further witnesses? You have heard the blasphemy. What is your opinion?' 'He is guilty.' they answered; 'he should die.'

Then they spat in his face and beat him with their fists; and others said, as they struck him, 'Now, Messiah, if you are a prophet, tell us who hit you.'

Meanwhile Peter was sitting outside in the courtyard when a serving-maid accosted him and said, 'You were there too with Jesus the Galilean.' Peter denied it in face of them all. 'I do not know what you mean', he said. He then went out to the gateway, where another girl, seeing him, said to the people there, 'This fellow was with Jesus of Nazareth.' Once again he denied it, saying with an oath, 'I do not know the man.' Shortly afterwards the bystanders came up and said to Peter, 'Surely you are another of them; your accent gives you away!' At this he broke into curses and declared with an oath: 'I do not know the man.' At that moment the cock crew. And Peter remembered how Jesus had said, 'Before the cock crows you will disown me three times.' He went outside, and wept bitterly.   *Matt. 26.59–75*

Peter became one of the founders of the Christian Church yet at one time he denied he even knew Jesus. This is the 'passion' or suffering of Jesus: none of his friends was prepared to stick with him in the time of his greatest need. Being left alone, friendless when you most need friends is what hurts most, more than attack by enemies, after all you expect enemies to be unkind and unpleasant.

Peter deserted Jesus in his time of need. There are many people today who are 'fair-weather' Christians; in a group of people who are hostile to Christianity they do not defend their Lord and their faith but join the attack. We all have a tendency to deny Christ in this way. Let us be warned by the experiences of Peter and accept the advice Jesus gave to him and all his followers: 'Watch and Pray'.

Let us pray:

O Lord Jesus Christ, look upon us with those eyes of thine, wherewith thou didst look upon Peter in the hall; that with Peter we may repent, and, by thy same love, be forgiven; for thine endless mercies sake. Amen.

BISHOP ANDREWES (adapted)

O Lord Jesus Christ, who hast called us to be thy soldiers and servants, grant that we may not be ashamed to confess Christ crucified, but may fight manfully under thy banner against sin, the world, and the devil, and continue thy faithful soldiers and servants unto our lives' end. Amen.

The Book of Common Prayer, (1662 *adapted*)

12. Saint Peter (ii) 'The Rock'

The season of Lent lasts for forty days when the Church prepares for Easter. The Church commemorates Easter for a further forty days after the event, which is quite rightly a time of rejoicing for Christians.

HYMN: *Come let us join our cheerful songs.*

Before Easter we heard about Peter's threefold denial that he ever knew Jesus. Peter had not heard the last of that though Jesus' subsequent death must have made Peter think so. One of the ten recorded occasions upon which Jesus was seen after the Resurrection by disciples was on the shores of Lake Galilee when Peter and a few others went back to their old jobs of fishing. Their Risen Master met them on the lake-side and breakfasted with them.

After breakfast, Jesus said to Simon Peter, 'Simon son of John, do you love me more than all else?' 'Yes, Lord,' he answered, 'you know that I love you.' 'Then feed my lambs', he said. A second time he asked, 'Simon son of John, do you love me?' 'Yes, Lord, you know I love you.' 'Then tend my sheep.' A third time he said, 'Simon son of John, do you love me?' Peter was hurt that he asked him a third time, 'Do you love me?' 'Lord,' he said, 'you know everything; you know I love you.' Jesus said, 'Feed my sheep.' *John 21.15–17*

Three times Peter is made to affirm his allegiance to Jesus. Each time Jesus, using the analogy of the shepherd, gives him more responsibility. Make no mistake it is a great responsibility to be a minister or vicar because people form their ideas about the whole church on what they hear the one minister they know say and what they see that one minister do. This is a great responsibility.

Let us pray for all ministers of religion, whether they are Roman Catholic priests, Church of England vicars, or Free Church ministers:

Almighty God, who by your son Jesus Christ gave to your apostle Peter many excellent gifts and commanded him to feed your flock; we ask you to make all ministers of religion careful and conscientious in preaching your holy word, throughout the world. We ask this in the name and for the sake of Jesus Christ Our Lord. Amen.

13. Saint Mark

Saints are usually regarded as absolutely perfect beings, and most of us consider we fall a long way short of being perfect and are thus unlikely to qualify for the title 'Saint'. In actual fact all the saints I have ever read about have been guilty of various sins, evils or wickedness at some time in their lives, but have also done a number of, or perhaps only one, really good deeds or deed. Saints are so called not only on account of their good deeds but despite the fact of their short comings.

This morning's hymn refers to God choosing ordinary fallible humans to work for him. The author of the hymn pleads that we might be roused from our state of apathy by their example.

HYMN: *Disposer supreme, and judge of the earth.*

A Saint who earned that title despite three rather glaring shortcomings is commemorated by the Church on 25 April. He was, to give him his full name, John Mark, the author of one of the four gospels.

His three shortcomings can be made to 'illuminate our spirits within' to quote the hymn we've just sung: that is, to teach us a thing or two.

First, Mark was present when Jesus was arrested in the Garden of Gethsemane, and like the others he ran away rather than risk arrest himself by protesting at Jesus' arrest. So he, though a follower of Christ, let him down when he needed help. Those of us who would call ourselves Christians also let Christ down in our lives by failing to defend Christ and Christianity from baseless attacks, when we could by a word correct a misapprehension, deny a rumour, or refute a falsehood.

Second, on Saint Paul's first missionary journey Mark deserted when they were about half-way. He didn't finish the job he'd promised to undertake. Another failing we are all too prone to: we leave a job half done.

And third, Greek scholars tell us that Mark's Gospel is written in poor Greek from the point of view of style and grammar. But Mark did his best, he felt he had a message to give to the world in writing and so he put it down in the best way he knew. No doubt he was painfully aware of the poor style and so on, but he went ahead all the same and Mark's Gospel is the favourite life-story of Jesus for many people.

Mark eventually became a bishop and a martyr and was accorded the title 'saint'; some good deeds . . . some shortcomings . . .

A message from Saint Mark's life for us is: what matters most is not what we have done in the past be it good or not so good, it is what we are doing in the present and whether or not we are trying to do what we know to be good and right to the best of our individual ability.

Let us pray:

Grant us, we beseech thee, O Lord, the aid of thy Holy Spirit that whatever by his teaching we know to be our duty, we may by his grace be enabled to perform; through Jesus Christ our Lord. Amen.

J. C. CHUTE: *A Book of Prayers for Schools*

14. Saint Alban

Bravery is a funny quality. It is often much easier for a person to do something dangerous or daring than for them to do something quite simple such as to say in front of disbelieving friends that they believe in God. Soldiers are all supposed to be brave or violent; so they might be, but soldiers are equipped with various devices for their defence. One of the first men to die for Christ in England had been a soldier, but he did not die as a soldier fighting in battle but as a civilian professing Christianity.

HYMN: *He who would valient be.*

During the first three hundred years of its existence the Christian Church was subject to sporadic attacks by the Roman State. The longest period of persecution lasted only seven years; but persecution could begin at any time. In the reign of the Emperor Diocletian England was part of the Roman Empire and because of an alleged threat to his throne by a Christian the Emperor ordered all subjects to worship the state Gods to demonstrate their loyalty. Christians all over the Empire refused and thousands died for their faith.

Alban had settled in the Roman town of Verulamium after he was 'de-mobbed' from the Roman Army. One day in AD 303 Alban gave shelter to a Welsh Christian priest called Amphibalus who was liable to execution on capture merely because he was a priest. Alban was impressed by the bravery of Amphibalus and was soon converted by him and baptised a Christian.

It was not long before the army in Verulamium learned that Alban was sheltering a priest. When the dreaded knock on the door came it was not the priest who was taken by the soldiers but Alban wearing Amphibalus' clothes. The deception was discovered at the trial but the only defence Alban uttered was 'I am a Christian and will ever worship Christ.' Despite a severe beating Alban would not deny Christ and was taken away and beheaded on a hill overlooking the river Ver. On the site of the execution now stands a great cathedral and the city is no longer called Verulamium but Saint Albans.

The year 303 was a long time ago but the bravery of Alban can be an example to us because his life and death show the true nature of bravery; to stand up for right against all odds. Some people say 'Why didn't he just say he believed in the Roman gods, save his life, and do more good by teaching others about Christ. You can't do that when you are dead can you?' The answer is 'Yes, you can!' If Alban had not stood his ground so bravely we should not know his name. His one costly action has inspired English people for 1,600 years to be brave for Christ.

Let us pray:

O Lord God, we thank you for the examples of true bravery which have been given to us by the martyrs of the Church. May we learn today from the example of Saint Alban, who was so impressed by the true bravery of the Christian priest that he too became a follower of Christ and who, though a soldier by training, used no weapon against his captors but said only, 'I am a Christian and will ever worship Christ'. We ask this in the name of Jesus, the master and example of all Christians, who himself faced suffering and death for the truth's sake. Amen.

15. Saint Swithin

Changes which constantly take place in nature sometimes bring pain and suffering to man and beast. In our hymn we recognise that nature is also beautiful and that there is love in the world as well as hatred. Beauty and love are regarded as attributes of God and hymn writers see in nature things for which they praise God.

HYMN: *For the beauty of the earth.*

In this country we are always grateful for a little sunshine and we usually curse the rain. This leads us to remember that today is the feast day of Saint Swithin. He was a bishop who died at Winchester in 862, having been bishop of the diocese for ten years and being much respected by two Kings of Wessex who rejoiced in the names of Egbert and Ethelwulf. In 971, over one hundred years after his death, he was made a saint. During the Middle Ages they were very superstitious and when the people annually paraded the relics (a polite religious word for what is usually a lot of old, three-quarter decayed bones) on 15 July it either rained and rained every day for weeks after; or it was sunny and remained so for weeks. Hence the superstition arose that whatever weather we have on Saint Swithin's day continues for forty days after.

A Greek writing in 320 BC, Theophrastus, wrote:

'Superstition seems to be simply cowardice about the supernatural.'

Perhaps we could add to that and say that it is also ignorance about the natural. Touching wood, throwing spilt salt over the shoulder, wearing Saint Christopher medallions and wearing crosses are superstitious practices. Excessive attention paid to superstitions is a very bad thing, because it leads to extreme conservatism and fear of anything new. It was superstition which prevented the men of the time from accepting Copernicus's proof that the earth was a revolving globe. Christianity and science combine to eliminate superstition in the twentieth century. The science of meteorology tells us that in summer most of our weather is dominated by belts of high pressure coming from Europe. Whatever weather they bring tends to last for a long time, so if it does rain on Saint Swithin's day then it is likely to continue. Likely, but not certain.

Science similarly explains other superstitions. Christianity accounts for the rest, because for the Christian the future, the unknown, and the supernatural offer no fears, no horrors, so there is nothing to be cowardly about. Cowardice and ignorance thus disposed of by Christianity and science render superstition a thing of the past not of the twentieth century.

Let us pray:

Almighty God, Maker of Heaven and earth, who hast given to us men not only eyes to see, but a mind to understand, the marvel of thy works; to search out thy secrets, and to discover thy hidden treasures: Quicken our conscience, we pray thee, as thou dost enlighten our understanding; and grant that in heart as in mind we may become daily more perfect, even as our Father in heaven is perfect; through Jesus Christ our Lord. Amen.

G. W. BRIGGS: *Daily Prayer*

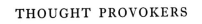

THOUGHT PROVOKERS

1. Angels

'I'm the greatest', said Cassius Clay. Mankind constantly regards himself as the greatest. 'There is no God', men say. 'There is no such thing as the devil.' 'Angels? Don't make me laugh!' Some scientists deny the possibility of life on the planet Jupiter. They are being egotistical because while it may be true that life as we know it on earth may not exist on Jupiter, for all we know there may be beings who enjoy H_2SO_4 as much as we do H_2O, who find temperatures of 7000 °C mild and spring-like. The planet Earth is a tiny part of one of the smallest galaxies in an infinite universe.

So there may be life of a completely different kind elsewhere in the universe. So why not angels? Angels are rational beings having free-will like ourselves but no bodies. When thinking of angels we immediately think of the Christmas Card and stained glass window type complete with haloes, feathers, and long white woolly nighties. None of the biblical references to angels describes them like this. When anything is said it is to do with shining light and that is all. Artists who wish to portray scenes involving angels have found it difficult to paint an invisible spirit without a body so they have given them bodies to symbolise their personalities, wings to symbolise their swiftness of movement and a long neutral robe to avoid making them appear to be of one or other sex and to emphasise their role as messengers of God.

The next question we have to answer is on what sort of occasion do they come into contact with men. Angels are agents of God who do things on his behalf. The four arch-angels have names which include the word 'el', which means 'God' in Hebrew, Mich-a-el—he who is like God, the warrior; Gabri-el—voice of

God, it was Gabriel who appeared to the Virgin Mary to tell her that she was going to be the mother of Jesus; Rapha-el—God has healed; and Uri-el—flame or fire of God, referring to the use of fire in purifying metal, for example.

Joseph was told by an angel first that it was all right to marry Mary and later that he should take Mary and Jesus to Egypt to escape Herod.

An angel appeared to Saint Peter to tell him to visit some Gentiles. Saint Stephen as he died was said to look like an angel. In the four Gospels there are about fifty references to angels.

Now we must ask, do they exist?

A recent article in a Christian magazine has said they do not. I can offer no proof; I have never seen one myself; but Jesus is often reported as having referred to angels in his teaching. What do they really look like? What do they do? How do they exist? These are all questions we are not able to answer. We cannot prove life on Jupiter, but neither can the scientists prove otherwise. Christ has said angels do exist, so the onus is on men who say they do not exist to prove they do not.

My mind is open but until evidence to the contrary is produced I will believe that there are angels.

Angels and men are constantly urged to unite in the praise of God and this we will now do in the words of a hymn.

HYMN: *All hail the power of Jesus' name.*

Let us pray:

May the Blessing of God Almighty, the Father, the Son and the Holy Spirit, rest upon us and upon our work and worship done in his name. May he give us light to guide us, courage to support us, and love to unite us, now and for evermore. Amen.

A Book of Prayers for Schools

2. The Bible

This morning we are to consider a difficulty which was raised by the author of Psalm 119 when he wrote 'Give me understanding that I may keep thy law.'

Obviously all who believe in one Absolute, All-powerful, All-knowing God will want to do what he suggests. Our difficulty is to understand what exactly God's laws are. The Holy Bible is certainly one source . . . but is it the *only* source of knowledge of God's will for man?

HYMN: *Lord, thy word abideth.*

'Oh that we, discerning it most holy learning.' To discern means to distinguish, to see something clearly in amongst other things. You cannot expect to flick open the Bible at any page and find a verse to settle your present problem, whatever it is. Nobody looks at only one square inch of a painting about four feet long by three feet high when deciding what value to set upon it. Similarly the Bible, if we are to derive benefit from it, if we are keen to *discern* God's laws for us, must be viewed as a whole, not in tiny bits. Individual stories, single verses, are only valuable when the full context is known. If we continue the painting analogy, we find the Bible a very long mural, stretching around the four walls of a very large room. It is possible to examine and derive benefit from looking at one wall or even part of one wall, but not single verses or half stories out of context. Again as with a painting parts of the Bible are very dull and have little of value to say to us. Part of our mural will consist of plain grey sky or big patches of grass, dull in themselves but important to the whole painting. So anybody who only looks at a Bible once every three years must not be surprised to find it useless in answering his problem. On the other hand the person who has studied, not just glanced at, all the Bible, Old and New Testaments, will know exactly where to turn when he needs guidance on a particular question.

The Bible does indeed contain 'holy learning' but not *all* is 'learning' and parts are far from 'holy' so we must be discerning. Most of us do not have the time to study all the Bible so we have to seek advice about which are the dull, irrelevant bits and we must also enquire about the background to the bits we do read.

It is quite unreasonable to believe that there is no writing which can help us with our understanding of God's law apart from the Bible. The authors of the various books of the Bible were undoubtedly inspired to write what they did. They did not write for the commercial market, nor for fame because so few could read what they wrote that it was a very poor business proposition. They wrote because they had something important to say. Despite the opportunity for making money by writing books today I am convinced that some modern authors are just as inspired by the Holy Spirit in their work as the Biblical authors.

Let us pray:

Almighty God, who hast made the people of this country members of one great body, we pray thee to bless all those who speak when many listen, and write what many read; Teach them that they may teach us, inspire them that they may inspire us, and grant that, thinking little of profit or fame, they may do their part to make the minds of people wise, their hearts sound, and their wills righteous, to the honour of Jesus Christ our Lord. Amen.

Boys' Prayer-Book (adapted)

3. Christian Aid

Jesus said: 'I give you a new commandment: Love one another: as I have loved you, so you are to love one another. If this love is among you, then all will know that you are my disciples.'

This is Christian Aid Week so let us pray for Christian Aid:

Heavenly Father, from whose Word we learn that by bearing one another's burdens we can fulfil the law of Christ: grant that through the work of Christian Aid we may bring comfort, hope and help to those whose needs are so much greater than our own. Give us the generous love of him who, though he was rich, became poor for us and for our salvation; and move the hearts of all who have it in their power to help to give gladly and freely for his sake, who gave himself to the uttermost for us, even Jesus Christ our Lord. Amen.

British Council of Churches: *Christian Aid*

With about half the world's population on or below subsistence level there is little need to explain why help of some sort is necessary, it should be given for two reasons:

First economic: people who have money can buy; those without cannot. Help people to become richer and you increase the potential market for goods.

Second, Christians are bound to love their neighbour and all the world is our neighbour.

Christian Aid is not an organisation for giving Bibles to the natives; it is not evangelistic. It helps *people*. In brief its methods are long term agricultural projects, sponsoring v.s.o. students, helping in disasters of all kinds with immediate gifts of whatever

F

is necessary, and trying to re-settle the thousands of refugees from the world's trouble spots. Christian Aid is run by the British Council of Churches which include all denominations except the Roman Catholic Church which has so far not joined the World Council of Churches though they send observers.

Christian Aid differs from Oxfam in that wherever there is a Christian community there is a ready-made organisation for administering the funds on the spot. There is no need to set up a special committee. Christian Aid is one of the most Christ-like of Church organisations because it is concerned with people as human beings and with their needs. Hungry people have no use for books. The hallmark of a Christian should not be his ability to find a biblical text for every occasion but his ability to help where and when needed. The Christian Church is setting an example to everybody in Christian Aid by forgetting their differences over doctrinal matters and doing together a useful piece of work.

Where do we come into this? By sheer chance we happened to be born in a part of the world which, in spite of freeze and squeeze, is quite well off. We all have more than one set of clothes, we each waste more food each lunch hour than many people have to live on for a week, there is not one of us who does not spend money on some non-essential item at least once a week. There is sufficient for everybody in the world to have enough. As we do pretty well we have a responsibility towards those who do not have anything like their fair share of the many good things of this world.

Let us pray:

O God our Father, in the name of him who gave bread to the hungry, we remember all who, through our human ignorance, folly, selfishness and sin, are condemned to live in want; and we pray that all endeavours for the overcoming of the world poverty and hunger may be so prospered that there may be food sufficient for all. We ask this through Jesus Christ our Lord. Amen.

British Council of Churches: *Christian Aid*

4. The Constancy of God

'O Lord, how manifold are thy works; in wisdom hast thou made them all; the earth is full of thy riches.'

HYMN: *Through all the changing scenes of life.*

'Through all the changing scenes of life.'
'How manifold are thy works.'

Everything in the world is in a perpetual state of change; ferns being squashed into coal; sea rising here, falling there, the Sahara was once a fertile area. Our lives too are subject to changes, one stage ends, another begins. This school year is nearly over, another one will begin all too soon.

Some of us will try to reform ourselves and make promises to do better, some will succeed, but as time goes on each of us has a bigger and more extensive past. Some try to live it down, some have to live up to it. Nothing stays the same, there is nothing we can be absolutely sure of. Only one thing, God is the same. God is perfect. That which is perfect cannot be improved. God is constant, but unlike the unfeeling mathematical constant, God cares. I have always found it a great help in the turmoil of life to know God exists and cares. I cannot prove his existence to anybody else; it is just what I believe; if somebody says to me 'I'm trying to believe but what about this. . . ', then explains the cause of his doubt, I can help because in my reading of philosophy, psychology, sociology, theology and all the other -ologies, I have met many of the written objections to a belief in God, and I continue to believe.

Anyhow I am convinced that a belief in God is beneficial; no, more than that, essential, to live in God's world to the full. There is nothing weak or cowardly about putting trust in God. A man who jumps from a plane at 30,000 feet and refuses to put his trust in a parachute is a raving nit. It is just as foolish to shun the help and guidance of Almighty God. 'Fear him, ye saints, and you will then have nothing else to fear,' or in other words 'Honour or respect him, you who would be Christians and you will then have nothing else to be frightened of.'

Let us pray:

O Almighty God, without beginning and without end, the Lord of thine own works: We praise and bless thee that thou gavest a beginning to time, and to the world in time, and to mankind in the world; and beseech thee so to dispose all men and all things that they may be gathered up in thee and thine endless heaven; through him who is the first and the last, Thy Son, our Saviour Jesus Christ. Amen.

G. W. BRIGGS: *Daily Prayer*

Eternal God, who changest not, as men change; who, though we be faithless, yet abidest faithful: Increase both our faith in the unchanging love of thy purpose, and our stedfastness in the doing of thy will; for Jesus Christ's sake. Amen.

G. W. BRIGGS: *Daily Prayer*

5. Daniel, the Courageous

In the fourth century before Christ, Alexander the Great spread Greek culture to all parts of the then known world. This naturally included the small but turbulent kingdom of Judah. It was not until a Greek called Antiochus Epiphanes became king over the Jews that any attempt was made at replacing the religion of the Jews by worship of the gods of the Greeks. A pro-Greek High Priest was appointed by this king and before long the Temple in Jerusalem was ordered to be used for the worship of the king of the Greek gods called Zeus; the Law of Moses was flouted; those who practised their religion were persecuted. Needless to say rebellion broke out led by Mattathias Maccabees and later by his son Judas, who asked all who cared anything for their beliefs to be prepared to fight, even to die for them.

HYMN: *Stand up, stand up for Jesus.*

In this situation in the year 165 BC a certain Jew wondered how he could encourage his fellow-country men to have the courage to stand up for their beliefs. Direct exhortation was too dangerous so he hit upon the idea of writing an historical novel whose hero was a man prepared to face death rather than deny his God. The hero was Daniel. The scene was set about 600 BC during the exile of the Jews in Babylon. Daniel had reached high office in the court of Darius the King of Persia.

> Then the presidents and the satraps sought to find a ground for complaint against Daniel with regard to the kingdom; but they could find no ground for complaint or any fault, because

he was faithful, and no error or fault was found in him. Then these men said, 'We shall not find any ground for complaint against this Daniel unless we find it in connection with the law of his God.'

Then these presidents and satraps came by agreement to the king and said to him, 'O King Darius, live for ever! All the presidents of the kingdom, the prefects and the satraps, the counsellors and governors are agreed that the king should establish an ordinance and enforce an interdict, that whoever makes petition to any god or man for thirty days, except to you, O king, shall be cast into the den of lions. Now O king, establish the interdict and sign the document, so that it cannot be changed, according to the law of the Medes and the Persians, which cannot be revoked.' Therefore King Darius signed the document and interdict.

When Daniel knew that the document had been signed, he went to his house where he had windows in his upper chamber open towards Jerusalem; and got down upon his knees three times a day and prayed and gave thanks before his God, as he had done previously. Then these men came by agreement and found Daniel making petition and supplication before his God. Then they came near and said before the king, concerning the interdict, 'O king! Did you not sign an interdict, that any man who makes petition to any god or man within thirty days except to you, O king, shall be cast into the den of lions?' The king answered, 'The thing stands fast, according to the law of the Medes and Persians, which cannot be revoked.' Then they answered before the king, 'That Daniel, who is one of the exiles from Judah, pays no heed to you, O king, or the interdict you have signed, but makes his petition three times a day.'

Then the king, when he heard these words, was much distressed, and set his mind to deliver Daniel: and he laboured till the sun went down to rescue him. Then these men came by agreement to the king, and said to the king, 'Know, O king, that it is a law of the Medes and Persians that no interdict or ordinance which the king establishes can be changed.' Then the king commanded, and Daniel was brought and cast into the den of lions. The king said to Daniel, 'May your God, whom you serve continually, deliver you!' And a stone was brought and laid upon the mouth of the den, and the king sealed it with his own signet and with the signet of his lords, that nothing might be changed concerning Daniel. Then the king went to his palace, and spent the night fasting; no diversions were brought to him, and sleep fled from him.

Then, at break of day, the king arose and went in haste to the den of lions where Daniel was, he cried out in a tone of anguish and said to Daniel, 'O Daniel, servant of the living God, has your God, whom you serve continually, been able to deliver you from the lions?' Then Daniel said to the king, 'O king, live for ever! My God sent his angel and shut the lions' mouths, and they have not hurt me, because I was found blameless before him; and also before you, O king, I have done no wrong,' Then the king was exceedingly glad, and commanded that Daniel be taken up out of the den. So Daniel was taken up out of the den, and no kind of hurt was found upon him, because he has trusted in his God.

Dan. 6.4–23

It is not important to discuss whether this is a true story or a figment of the author's imagination, Daniel certainly had some 'guts'. He was not to know that he would survive the punishment fixed for those who offended against the 'interdict' when he stuck loyally to his God and his faith. Do we show the same loyalty to our beliefs or do we waver in the face of opposition or ridicule? Let us try and emulate Daniel and always have the courage of our convictions to do what we know to be right at all times.

Let us pray:

Lord and King, we pray thee for courage to face unpopularity for the sake of truth; for courage to declare boldly our convictions, though they make us despised; for courage to break with evil custom and evil opinions. Give us strong hearts that will not fear what any man may do to us. Give us, O Lord, the spirit of boldness, that being delivered from all fear of our fellows, we may be strong in thee, and very courageous; through Jesus Christ our Lord. Amen.

J. S. HOYLAND: *A Book of Prayers for Schools* (adapted)

6. Examinations

A nineteenth-century author wrote:

> 'Examinations are formidable even to the best prepared, for the greatest fool may ask more than the wisest man can answer.'

HYMN: *O Jesus I have promised.*

Two schoolboys left school when they were fifteen before taking any public exams. One, Roy, was quite bright but could not see the point of school, he knew that in the local factory he could earn ten pounds a week even at fifteen and the older men were able to earn thirty or forty pounds and some of them left school when they were twelve. The other fellow, Ian, was usually pretty near the bottom of the class in most subjects except Art and woodwork. His father owned the local factory and promised him a job there helping to run the factory as soon as he could leave school.

A few years later Roy was *quite* happy; he was earning fifteen pounds a week, with overtime, but the job was rather monotonous. 'Not enough responsibility', he said. Ian too was pretty content, he had an office of his own. Dad had fixed it. He did not understand quite what he was doing but he muddled through. Recently Roy has become very dissatisfied with life; he could not get promotion; it went to people with better qualifications; he still did the same old job; day after day; he was bored to tears. As for Ian, well his muddles got bigger and bigger; he dare not admit he couldn't understand and eventually he had a nervous breakdown and has been in hospital for the last six months.

F*

What has all this to do with exams? The way society runs at present it is not unusual for several hundred people to apply for one job. It would take too long to interview each individual so the simplest way seems to be to choose the ones with the best paper qualifications, most 'O' levels, 'A' levels et cetera. Now though exams are not perfect it is somewhat better than picking names out of a hat. Roy would find it much easier to get a job to satisfy him if he had a few certificates to show to would-be employers. As for Ian, if he had been allowed to stay at school both he and his father would have discovered that Ian was not cut out for heavy managerial responsibilities but he could have developed his talents in Art and Woodwork and may have become a famous sculptor or cabinet-maker.

That then is the function of public examinations: to help people gauge their own and others' ability. There may be faults with the system but what the examiner wants to know is what you know about a subject, not what you do not know. As those exams are important to people's lives it is essential that they have some practice before the ones that really matter as we have school exams.

Each of us has different interests and abilities or what the New Testament calls talents. The message of the teaching of Jesus in the New Testament is that we should use such ability as we have to the full; for some that may mean being university professors of physics, for others entertaining by singing or dancing. Whatever our particular talent may be it is a gift of God and should be developed and trained and used to try and make the world a better place for our having lived in it.

Let us pray:

Almighty God, guide and bless all those who will be sitting for examinations in these coming weeks that they may have calmness and good tempers, a sound judgment in all things, freedom from fuss and strain in the face of unusual conditions, and, if it be thy will, success. This we ask in the name of Jesus Christ Our Lord. Amen.

A Book of Prayers for Schools

7. Faith

Bertrand Russell wrote:

'Faith is the belief in that for which there is no evidence.'

We read in the Epistle to the Hebrews:

'Faith gives substance to our hopes, and makes us certain of realities we do not see.

The word 'faith' is sometimes used as an alternative for the word 'religion'; the Jewish faith, the Muslim faith. This morning our thoughts are going to be about faith, its meaning, its purpose and its importance.

HYMN: *Fight the good fight with all thy might.*

When there is abundant evidence for the existence of something or other we can truly say we *know* it exists or is true. For example, I know that this platform on which I am standing actually exists, that it is there. It is not possible for me to hover four feet above you without some sort of assistance. I am not suspended from a wire so I must be supported from beneath. This is an example of *knowledge*. Now if I say I believe you are all listening to me at this moment it may be true but it is not necessarily true just because I am here talking and you are there, each possessing an efficient pair of ears. I could find out, I suppose, by asking everybody to write an account of what I have said, then I could say I knew that *X* was listening or that I knew *Y* was not. But at this moment I do not know. I could, then, have faith that you are listening and I could prove it true or false given time.

With regard to belief in God his existence cannot be proved in the same way that the existence of the platform can be proved. People have faith in God . . . , they believe he exists, and cares, and loves. Faith is a leap in the dark each individual must attempt for himself.

One day I shall *know* whether God exists or not. When I die if there is 'nothing' then I was wrong, not that I shall be aware of my error, but if there is 'something' I shall *know*. What is important is that if I were to know what happened after death I could adjust my behaviour accordingly. If there was 'nothing' I might be out to enjoy myself as much as possible without caring what happened to other people, merely making sure I was not caught doing anything against the law. As it happens I have faith in God and this belief leads me to adjust my living so that I try to conform to the will of God, to love him and to love my neighbour as myself.

Faith, for the Christian, is belief in God, the Father, Son, and Holy Spirit. Its purpose is to make sense of life on earth for him, and its importance is that it has a fundamental affect on the way in which he acts in his life.

> 'Only believe, and thou shalt see
> That Christ is all in all to thee.'

Only when one believes in Christ can one know what it is like to believe. Nobody who has *really* believed ever stops believing. It is bewildering for the non-believer; dare he make the necessary leap? Only when he is dead will he have enough evidence to *know*, then it will be too late. It is now or never. It takes courage to be a Christian because there can be no logically valid, scientifically sound, intellectually reasonable grounds for the belief, it is a single, naked, lonely act of faith.

Let us pray:

O Holy Spirit, grant us, we pray thee, the gift of courage. Enable us to live as Jesus lived, in steadfast opposition to sin and in courageous faith in the power of God. As Jesus faced the hatred of enemies and the desertion of friends on earth, so may we be prepared to face manfully and with unfailing faith whatever opposition or enmity our service of Christ may arouse against us, in certain hope that in all things we can be strengthened through him who has overcome the world even Jesus Christ Our Lord. Amen.

E. M. VENABLES: *Sons of God*

8. Friendship

In an essay on friendship Ralph Emerson wrote in about 1870

'A friend is a person with whom I may be sincere.'

HYMN: *O Jesus I have promised.*

This is the age of the 'instant'; instant this . . . , instant that . . , Nesquik . . . , Blend 37 . . . , Nescafé . . Maxwell House . . , Sainsbury's Special . . . , Instant Whip . . . . Quite reasonable-tasting things ready in a flash. Paintings done in a trice; just apply water and there you are—a perfect picture. Pre-fabricated buildings. Every department of life is, or so it seems, dominated by speed. But there are exceptions; you cannot have instant friendship, instant marriage. Friends grow together, you learn more about people you meet, to understand them; the relationship develops from people you have met, to acquaintances, to friendship. So you cannot have instant friendship, nor can you have instant God. People say 'Perhaps there's something in this God lark!' So they go to church once, perhaps twice, and for good measure they even say a couple of prayers. Then they give it all up, they do not get anything out of it. What about religious conversion? Well, that is only a beginning. One can fall in love at first sight but one still has to cultivate the friendship. A relationship with God is fostered in the same way. Daily private prayer is chatting to God, as you chat to friends; public worship is visiting his house as you visit friends' homes. Friends are always keen to find out more about each other so they can understand each other better. Those who would be friends of God can find out a lot about him from reading various parts of the Bible. This is why daily reading is recommended.

As you speak to others about your friends and defend them if attacked, so the friend of God does these things for God; true friends do things for each other. Jesus said 'Whatever you do to these you do for me' In this way Jesus Christ really becomes our Master and our Friend.

Let us pray:

Lord Jesus we remember that you call all your disciples on earth your friends we ask that we might be worthy to be considered some of your friends. We ask you to bless our earthly friendships that they may be happy and kept pure. And for our part we promise to do our utmost to keep our friendship with you in good repair through prayer, Bible reading and living lives after the example you gave us on earth. Amen.

May the blessing of God Almighty, the Father, the Son, and the Holy Spirit, be with us and remain with us this day and for ever. Amen.

9. Race

On 20 November 1963 the General Assembly of the United Nations unanimously adopted this 'Declaration of the elimination of all forms of racial discrimination' which states in Article one:

'Discrimination between human beings on the grounds of race, colour or ethnic origin is an offence to human dignity.'

Our hymn states categorically that Christianity also regards racial discrimination as an offence to human dignity 'People and realms of *every* tongue Dwell on his love . . . '

HYMN: *Jesus shall reign where'er the sun.*

Even a scanty knowledge of the Old Testament shows a curious mixture of genial tolerance and unrelenting intolerance of other nations by the Children of Israel. Isaiah looked forward to the time when all nations would worship God in Jerusalem while Ezra forbade intermarriage on pain of death. The grandmother of King David, Ruth, was a Moabitess, a foreigner.

When we turn to the New Testament we notice that most of Jesus' dealings were with Jews but there are enough incidents recorded to show that Jesus was in no way prejudiced against non-Jews. He healed the servant of a Roman Centurion and the daughter of a Syro-Phoenician woman. It was no accident that the hero of his most famous parable was a Samaritan. The story was told in answer to the question 'who is my neighbour?' Jesus' answer means in effect 'Anybody; absolutely *any* other human being who needs your help, he is your neighbour.' This teaching is carried on by Saint Paul who says that within Christianity questions of being Greek, or Roman, or Jewish, or a slave or a freeman are just not relevant.

Of course, foreigners are different; they dress differently, speak differently have different cutsoms. I have several ties; they are all different but I like them all and they are all ties. There are some ties which I do not possess, some which I dislike and would not want anyway. In the same way there are nasty dirty, criminal black people as well as intelligent, hard-working, pleasant ones. But there are also nasty, dirty, criminal white people. In assessing the value of a human being his race or skin colour has no more relevance than the colour of his eyes or indeed the length of his hair. Research into 'spare-part surgery' has underlined the fact that a human being is basically the same regardless of race, colour or sex. The blood groups of Nigerians are the same as the groups found among Russians.

The United Nations, and 1,900 years before it Jesus Christ, condemned discrimination on the grounds of race. This applies to the Western and Northern Nigerian treatment of the Ibo of Biafra, to the Kenyan treatment of Asians, to relations between Indians and Pakistanis as well as to the attitude we white English have towards the Irish, the Poles, the French besides the West Indians, Chinese and any other so-called coloured person.

The only law which will eliminate such prejudices is the law of love of Jesus Christ who called all men to be his brothers.

Let us pray:

O God, who hast made of one blood all nations to dwell upon the earth, break down, we beseech thee, all that divides us one from another; shame our jealousies, and lay low our pride; do away with all race-prejudice, that the bonds of fellowship and mutual service may unite the east and the west, the north and the south, that we may live in peace together, in honour preferring one another; to the glory of thy Name. Amen.

G. C. BINYON (adapted)

10.   The Sea

This morning I want us to think about the sea, ourselves and Christianity.

HYMN: *Eternal Father, strong to save.*

When Christianity was a secret society, in the days when by being a Christian one risked one's life, the code sign was a fish. Several of Jesus' apostles were fishermen. Jesus taught from a boat on several occasions. He spoke of catching men and of sorting good fish from the bad. Yet the Jewish people feared the sea. The sudden storms of Galilee and the breadth of the Mediterranean un-nerved them. One of the Psalmists writes:

> See the works of the Lord,
> And his wonders in the deep.
> For he commandeth and raiseth the stormy wind,
> Which lifteth up the waves thereof.
> They mount up to the heaven, they go down again to the depths:
> Their soul is melted because of trouble.
> They reel to and fro, and stagger like a drunken man,
> And are at their wit's end.
>
> *Psalm 107.24–27*

The Channel Tunnel is not yet built so we in England are very dependent upon men whose daily work is on the sea. Much of our food is imported from abroad; we owe our weekly ration of fish-fingers to sailors; our island has, especially in the past, been easy to defend while our sailors have had command of the sea. A storm at sea is just as unpleasant in 1968 as it was in 1068 or

164

68 or in 1068 BC when Saul was King of Israel. During the winter months especially let us occasionally spare a thought and a prayer for the men who earn their living by working on the sea.

Some of you will say, no doubt, that's their fault if they choose to go to sea, but we can still afford to be grateful to them. One can also think of their families and the anxiety their wives and children must suffer when storms rage.

If we may relate the sea again to ourselves and our religion it is interesting how we talk of 'ports in storms'. 'havens of rest', 'the sea of life' and so on. Some people drift along but others use their religion as an anchorage and the teaching of Jesus Christ as a chart. This is a course which I recommend.

Let us pray:

O Eternal Lord God, who alone spreadest out the heavens and rulest the raging of the sea; Be pleased to receive into thy almighty and most gracious protection all sailors and the ships in which they sail. Preserve them from the dangers of the sea, that they may reach in safety the lands to which they go, and with a thankful remembrance of thy mercies may praise and glorify thy holy name: through Jesus Christ our Lord. Amen.

The Book of Common Prayer, 1662 (adapted)

11. Vocation

HYMN: *Father, hear the prayer we offer.*

Many people have claimed and still do claim to have been called by God to do some particular work in the world. Though this is called '*vocation*' most people who say they have been called have not actually heard the voice of God sounding in their ears. Straight away that statement needs qualification by saying that Joan of Arc was convinced she heard voices telling her how she could lead the French to victory over the English. (At her trial she admitted that the voices may only have been figments of her imagination but they were sufficiently vivid to have an amazing effect upon her life and on France and even on the history of Europe). One can also point to the Old Testament where it is clearly recorded that Moses, Samuel, Elijah and Isaiah for example held conversations with God. The thing to notice in these stories is not the direct speech aspect but that the men where somehow persuaded to do something they had originally intended not to do. Moses fled from Egypt, Elijah fled from Samaria, Samuel and Isaiah were given unenviable tasks of warning about unpleasant events likely to take place.

Also worth noting about these four examples is the diversity of their backgrounds. Moses was a refugee turned shepherd, Samuel a young lad training to be a priest, Elijah a solitary hermit shunning society and Isaiah a nobleman who held high positions in the court of the King of Judah. This diversity of background is the first thing we can learn from these four. Anybody can be called by God to do some task.

Vocation is usually used to describe the acceptance of God's instruction for a long-term project; maybe a whole life's work, rather than a daily duty sheet issued by God. As I mentioned a moment ago not everybody is called directly by God speaking to them. There are three other ways in which one can become aware of the fact that God has a particular task for you.

First, there is that inner feeling that we ought to do such-and-such; nothing else seems to be satisfactory. It was this inner feeling that drove Wilberforce to persevere in his work of abolishing the slave trade.

Second, other people can say in all seriousness 'You ought to do this job; you'd do it well' or 'You're cut out to be a teacher, minister, doctor or whatever.' Make no mistake it's not only ministers who are called to do work for God; as Saint Paul made quite clear there are many different sorts of gifts which can be exercised in the service of God.

Third, one can be called by the course that events take. Things happen which seem to make it obvious what you yourself ought to do.

A further point is that vocation is a two-way process. God makes the effort to contact people but vocation is not complete until the person has responded. Your mother can shout her head off for you to come to tea and you may not respond because you are either out of earshot, or making too much noise to hear her, or just not prepared to take any notice though you have heard. Similarly one can fail to hear the call of God, in whatever form it takes, by never thinking about God or by being so concerned with asking for things in prayer that God can't get a word in edgeways, or by deliberately deciding not to do what you feel called to do because it seems difficult or there's no money in it.

My plea to you is firstly be mentally and spiritually alert to any call or vocation which may be coming your way, and secondly be very careful over what you say and think about the vocations other people claim to have. Because some people never find their vocation it does not mean that it is not a very real experience for others.

Let us pray:

We pray not, O Lord our God, that thou shouldest reveal thyself by outward signs of mighty works, but in the quiet solitude of our inmost heart; not by the thunder and the lightning, but by the still small voice; and when thou speakest, give, we beseech thee, to thy servants the hearing ear, and a heart to obey; though Jesus Christ our Lord. Amen.

G. W. BRIGGS: *Daily Prayer*

12. War

'That war is an evil is something we all know, and it would be pointless to go on cataloguing all the disadvantages involved in it.' When was that written? In yesterday's newspaper? No! After the Korean War? No! Not even after either of the World Wars. The man who wrote this statement lived more than four centuries before Christ! But besides its horrors every war seems to produce its crop of heroes.

HYMN: *Onward Christian Soldiers.*

Whether I am reading history or the daily paper I am struck by two facts about war which seem to be independent of time. First there is the barbarity of war. How can men do such things to their fellows! There is little to choose between the tortures inflicted upon Christians in the Roman Empire in the early three-hundreds and the German concentration camps of the last World War. Religious wars have abounded; the Spaniards slaughtered thousands in South America in the name of God; the Tudors of England each produced their spate of martyrs: Sir Thomas More, Archbishop Cranmer and Edmund Campion, each died under a different Tudor monarch for their religion.

So much for the debit side. The other fact that strikes me is the way in which war seems to bring the best out of so many people. The ideals of Christian Knighthood were a *result* of the Crusades; Florence Nightingale owes her fame to a war; Gladys Aylward, the Small Woman, was inspired in the midst of war between China and Japan to practise and to preach Christianity in China. The horrors of war-time Nazi prison camps brought many men and women face to face with the problem of their own faith and through prison they became Christians and worked and often sacrificed themselves for fellow prisoners.

Here we have the problem; it is a paradox. War brings both the best and the worst out of people. This statement seems to contradict itself but history shows it to be true. Two conclusions can be drawn from this. One is to the effect that every so often we need a war to give opportunities to those people who are improved by adversity. One can produce other reasons to support this conclusion such as saying war keeps the population down and gives incentive to inventors whose work can have peaceful uses as well as destructive. Atomic power is often quoted as an example here. Whole nations can let off steam in a war; crime and juvenile delinquency are reduced in war-time.

The alternative conclusion says that war is utterly wrong. It may be the lesser of two evils as the Archbishop of Canterbury in 1939 stated, but as he also emphasised war is very definitely evil. Confronted with such evils as war inevitably brings, individuals are shocked out of their complacency into doing something positive to relieve suffering; so good does come out of war but the cause is man's determination to do good; war is only the stimulus.

Surely enlightened man of the second half of the twentieth century can act for the good of others without waiting for the horrible and destructive stimulus of war bullying him into it. Through Christianity it *is* possible; Christians do 'march as to war'. The enemy is disease, pain, want, suffering, every evil in the world. Who can fail to volunteer for such an army!

Let us pray:

Almighty God, give us grace to contend always for what is true and right, and to be ready if need be to suffer for it. Give us not over to any death of the soul, but rather lift us into newness of life, and let us glorify and enjoy thee for ever; through Jesus Christ our Lord. Amen.

A Book of Prayers for Schools

ACKNOWLEDGEMENTS

The thanks of the author and publishers are due to the following publishers for permission to quote extracts:

British Council of Churches, *Thoughts and Prayers for Christian Aid Week;* T. & T. Clark, *Communion with God* by Darwell Stone and David Simpson; Faber and Faber Ltd., 'Innocents' Day' from *The Pot Geranium* by Norman Nicholson; Longmans Green & Co. Ltd., *Prayers for the City of God* by G. C. Binyon; John Murray, *A Chain of Prayer Across the Ages* by Selina Fox; Oxford University Press, *Daily Prayer*, compiled by Eric Milner-White and G. W. Briggs; SCM Press, *A Book of Prayers for Schools.*

Thanks are also due to Professor William Barclay for permission to use one of his prayers from *The Plain Man's Book of Prayers.* The extract from the *Revised Standard Version of the Bible* is copyrighted by the Division of Christian Education, National Council of Churches of Christ in the U.S.A. and used by permission.

Extracts from the *New English Bible* copyright 1961 are used by permission of the Oxford and Cambridge University Presses.

The Book of Common Prayer of 1662 is Crown copyright and extracts quoted herein are with permission.

An extract from the *Prayer Book as Proposed in 1928* is printed with the permission of the Holders of the copyright.

Should any copyright have been omitted inadvertently then this oversight will be rectified in subsequent editions.